Training for Rock Climbing

CW00954337

Training for Rock Climbing

Steve Bollen

Fully endorsed by
the British Mountaineering Council

Pelham Books
LONDON

PELHAM BOOKS

Published by the Penguin Group
27 Wrights Lane, London W8 5TZ
Viking Penguin Inc., 375 Hudson Street, New York, New York 10014, USA
Penguin Books Australia Ltd, Ringwood, Victoria, Australia
Penguin Books Canada Ltd, 10 Alcorn Avenue, Toronto, Ontario, Canada M4V 3B2
Penguin Books (NZ) Ltd, 182–190 Wairau Road, Auckland 10, New Zealand

Penguin Books Ltd, Registered Offices: Harmondsworth, Middlesex, England

First published in 1994
First published in this paperback edition March 1997
Copyright © Steve Bollen 1994

Typeset in Monophoto Times $11\frac{1}{2}$/13pt
by Selwood Systems, Midsomer Norton
Printed and bound in Great Britain by
Butler & Tanner Ltd, Frome and London

A CIP catalogue record for this book is available from the British Library

ISBN 0 7207 2035 4

The moral right of the author has been asserted

To my very patient wife,
and ideal climbing partner,
Christina

Contents

Introduction

Why have I written this book? As an orthopaedic surgeon with a special interest in sports injuries, I have to have a thorough understanding of training methods and regularly see, and have to deal with, the effects of bad or inappropriate training in many sports. More particularly, as the medical adviser to the British Mountaineering Council, I have been in a unique position to see a large number of climbers who have been injured, at least 50 per cent of whom have been injured while training. As a besotted rock climber myself, I am able to analyse and understand what is needed by today's rock athletes.

At the present time there is little in the way of guidance for the aspiring climber as to the best way to train, both to improve performance and at the same time avoid injury. In these days of proliferating competitions and ever increasing standards on the crag, it is unlikely that pure talent can take anyone to the top, and therefore training is now an essential part of any committed climber's day-to-day routine.

Training is not just for the stars of our sport, however. We all have potential which most of us never get anywhere near realising. Training can improve anyone's climbing from the V.diff beginner to the competition king (or queen). You can improve strength, endurance, skill or even the ability to deal with those dreadful thoughts about death or mutilating injury that tend to creep unbidden into your head when ten metres above your last poor RP and facing a ground fall if you fail the crux! All it requires is the will to improve, time in which to train and the self discipline to keep going when it is cold, you've had a hard day at work, there's something good on the television, etc., etc.

You may ask, if I know so much about training, why am I not world cup champion or at least climbing 6C? There's an old coaching saying, 'You can't put in what God left out,' and we can't all climb like Jerry Moffat. My talents lie elsewhere but that doesn't stop me dreaming and working at the weights and at the climbing wall on those long, dark winter evenings, with the thoughts of next year's routes spurring me on...

I have written this book to try and help anyone who is a climber and wants to improve with the minimum risk of injury. There is at present no scientifically proven, cast-iron guaranteed programme to make you climb 7A, but there are many hard-won lessons from other sports that can be applied to climbing. It is obviously impossible to give specific regimes to cover all the different demands of many different individuals, but I hope you will find enough information here to plan a training programme that will produce the desired result.

1   General Principles

This book is organised so that each chapter should logically progress from the previous one. Some key points will be repeated in different sections (as it is said you have to read something three times to remember it, this may be no bad thing!)

I will start with an overview of some of the basic principles in training theory. These will be further expanded upon in the relevant sections as you read on.

Training is a manipulation of the body's physiology, in an attempt to improve performance. It is the quality of training, not the mere quantity, that is the first important point. If you train badly, you will not only fail to make the gains you hope for, you may also permanently damage yourself, or at least spend a lot of time getting to know the local sports clinic physiotherapist!

FREQUENCY

How often should you train? This will obviously depend on a number of factors, such as time available, commitment etc., but, as a general rule, to make any gains one should train at least twice a week, and to make gains more quickly, three to four times a week is preferable. This does not just mean training sessions, but the training of the particular muscle groups involved in a particular set of exercises. Bearing this in mind, it is possible to train every day without overdoing it, providing different groups of muscles are exercised on successive days – this is known as a split routine.

There is a lot of evidence that training sessions are best split into two. Top-class athletes tend to have a training session in the morning (two hours after breakfast), a rest in the middle of the day, and then train again in the late afternoon. Training sessions are usually one-and-a-half to two hours long, making a total (if you are full time) of three or four hours a day. If you start training for much longer than this, your body cannot recover sufficiently between sessions, leading into a downward spiral of fatigue and injury.

Resting is a very important part of training schedules. After a particularly gruelling session or climb, it will take forty-eight hours for the body to recover its peak potential. Not allowing the body to recover, and then repeating the abuse, inevitably results in decrease in performance and possible overuse injury.

It is now recognised that it is possible to chronically overtrain. In women this can result in irregularities or even complete cessation of the menstrual cycle (see Chapter 10). In both men and women it can affect the immune system, resulting in a susceptibility to infection. This is why many top athletes become ill around competition time, just as they are trying to 'peak'. Obviously there is a fine line between training maximally and overtraining, although this can be monitored by weekly blood counts, checking the function of the white cells. For most of us, however, the problems of overtraining are unlikely to arise!

SPECIFICITY

It is important that, if you are going to train, you concentrate on the muscles that are used in climbing. Although this seems obvious, and that doing thousands of pull ups is the right way to go, in reality the situation is more subtle than it first appears.

Most individual muscles do their work in partnership with the muscle that performs the opposite movement, called the antagonist. For instance the biceps, which bends your arm up at the elbow, is paired with the triceps, which straightens the arm out. When you have a weight in your hand and bend your arm up, as the biceps is contracting, the triceps is actively relaxing (this sounds paradoxical but means that, although it is being stretched, it is paying out the tension), producing a carefully controlled movement.

It is well documented that in sprinters an imbalance between the quadriceps on the front of the thigh and the hamstrings on the back of the thigh increases the chance of injury, and there are many other similar examples in other sports. In practical terms this means that one should not only train the specific muscles involved in a particular action but also the muscles that perform the opposite movement (the antagonists), aiming to achieve muscle balance around a particular joint.

In order for some muscles to work to their maximum advantage, it is necessary that the joint around which they work is held in a stable position. This is particularly important around the shoulder where the muscles that hold the shoulder blade are often neglected and, if not corrected, this can produce pain in the front part of the shoulder or between the shoulder blades (see Chapter 10).

In summary, one has to train the specific muscles involved in climbing, plus their antagonists, plus the stabilisers of the joints involved, in order to maximise performance and minimise the chances of injury.

PROGRESSIVE OVERLOAD

This is the basic principle for improving muscular strength. One of the earliest examples of this technique comes from ancient Greece, where wrestlers training for the games were advised to pick up a new-born bull and train by lifting it every day as it grew larger and larger. Your body adapts to the stresses put upon it and will only change if the strains put upon it increase or decrease. To gain in strength, one must adopt a training schedule placing loads in excess of that to which the body has become accustomed, and exercise to the point of muscle failure. This point will change and progress as you reap the benefits of your programme.

It is a mistake to progress too far too fast, however, as muscles gain strength much more rapidly than their associated tendons, leading to an increased risk of injury at the musculo-tendinous junction. It takes a tendon six weeks to catch up with each significant gain in muscular strength, so take things steadily.

BASIC AEROBIC FITNESS

It is now well established that a basic level of aerobic fitness is essential for good performance in virtually all sports. It also makes you feel better, improves your immune system etc. The bad news is this means thirty minutes of jogging, cycling, aerobics or swimming three times a week as a basic minimum.

FORWARD PLANNING

Most high-class athletes have their training programmes planned out well in advance, usually based on four-year cycles around the Olympic games. This will take into account intervening competitions and will be devised so as to peak at the appropriate times.

For most of us mere mortals, for whom competition climbing is an unlikely problem, planning may not be quite so critical, but there may well be routes targeted for next season for which certain aspects of training may make the vital difference between success and failure. For the average climber in the UK the 'training season' is usually in the long, cold, dark winter months from November to April, and you can plan your programme to emerge fully fit, with your new and powerful physique, in the spring.

FIND A PARTNER

It is often difficult to maintain the enthusiasm for a long-term training programme in the face of so many of the distractions society has to offer! A regular training partner makes it that much more difficult to wimp out. They can also offer encouragement and support (or abuse) and make training to muscle failure with weights or on the wall a safer proposition (see Chapter 5).

2 Muscles, Tendons and Ligaments

This chapter will give you some idea about the parts of your body you are trying to change and at the same time avoid injuring.

I'm sure you will have a rough idea about the basic structure of the bony skeleton. The skeleton serves two purposes: it protects some of the vital organs, such as the brain, heart, lungs and abdominal organs; and it provides anchoring and insertion points for the various muscles, tendons and ligaments that move you around.

MUSCLES

There are about four hundred individual muscles in the body, making up roughly 45 per cent of total body mass, but only seventy-five pairs of these muscles are responsible for maintaining posture and producing the movements of arms and legs required for climbing.

There are three different sorts of muscles, made up of distinct fibre types – cardiac, smooth and skeletal. Cardiac and smooth muscles are responsible for the jobs which require continuous and independent action, as found in the heart and walls of the intestines. It is skeletal muscle (muscle that you have active control over) and how to manipulate it to improve strength, power and endurance that we are largely concerned with in this book.

Each muscle is made up of numerous muscle fibres, which are themselves made up of a number of striated myofibrils. At a microscopic level, each myofibril is made up of a chain of sarcomeres which are the basic contractile units of muscle. Within each sarcomere are two types of protein molecule, actin and myosin.

This sounds terribly complicated but basically actin and myosin are arranged in a sort of molecular ratchet system. As a muscle contraction is initiated, they slide between one another, breaking and remaking molecular bonds and shortening the sarcomere. If you can imagine this occurring along the long chain of sarcomeres making up a myofibril, then repeated within all the myofibrils in a muscle fibre and then all the muscle fibres contracting at the same time, you can see what makes your biceps shorten and bulge as you strike that pose for the photos.

Skeletal muscles are themselves made up of several different types of fibre but there are broadly speaking two distinct types which perform different functions. 'Slow twitch' fibres, which are responsible for aerobic endurance, and 'fast twitch' fibres, which produce more force but tire more rapidly. It is said that the proportions of these fibre types within an individual's muscles may be genetically determined, and this is the reason why one person excels as a marathon runner and another as a sprinter. At the present time, however, the evidence is equivocal as to whether it is genetics or training that is the most important influence.

We do know that slow twitch fibres are made up of long sarcomeres, so there are fewer of these in series within an individual myofibril, resulting in a relatively slow contraction. Fast twitch fibres have much shorter sarcomeres and therefore have many more in series within a myofibril. This means they are capable of much faster and explosive contraction. Oxygen is a key component in muscle contraction, although muscles can work for short periods without it. The actual chemical reactions required to produce the energy for muscle contraction in the presence of oxygen are quite complicated and, if you are interested, can be found in a biology text book under the 'Krebs cycle'.

When muscles are working at a rate at which the supply of oxygen can be maintained at an adequate level, they are said to be working 'aerobically'. The length of time that they can be kept going is then dependent on energy reserves, the efficiency of the muscle enzyme systems in utilising the fuels of fatty acids and glucose, and the efficiency of the heart and lungs in delivering oxygen. These factors can all be influenced by training. For example, anyone who has started jogging knows that, as the days and weeks go by, the distance you feel comfortable with slowly increases, and the effort required becomes less and less.

Once you start to put in a bit more effort and the body can no longer deliver oxygen to the working muscles fast enough, even by increasing the heart and respiratory rates, then muscles start working 'anaerobically'. This form of energy production is much less efficient than the aerobic system and produces byproducts such as lactic acid which, when they build up enough, actually inhibit muscle contraction. These byproducts produce the burning sensation as your forearms slowly pump out and your fingers uncurl. Training both increases your tolerance to, and possibly increases your ability to remove, the harmful byproducts of this form of energy production.

Muscles produce their force by contraction and can act in one of three ways. In 'isometric' contraction there is no actual movement of the body or the object you are trying to move and the muscle involved retains the same overall length. This happens when statically holding on to an undercut or when locked off on a hold. It can be used as a method of exercise in the early stages when recovering from injury and is useful at the beginning of a warm up.

'Concentric' contraction occurs when the muscle shortens while producing a force. The biceps during the first phase of a biceps curl or your latissimus dorsi during a pull up are good examples of this sort of action. It is usually this action you are working on when trying to develop explosive power.

'Eccentric' contraction occurs when the muscle lengthens while still producing a force. This occurs when lowering under control from a pull up, or lowering the weight from a biceps curl. It is eccentric use of muscles that is mainly responsible for producing muscle soreness (see injury chapter) and is the most important muscle action that you need to control in order to prevent injury. For instance, going up a Bachar ladder using concentric contractions does not usually cause injury, it is the coming down, when you drop on to your arm, producing a 'shock load' eccentric contraction, that causes the damage. A predominantly eccentric exercise programme is often used when rehabilitating from tendinitis and overuse injuries. There is also some evidence that it is the eccentric component of exercise that is the most powerful stimulus to increasing muscle strength.

TENDONS

Muscles exert their force through their tendons. These are the tough fibrous cords, made up from collagen, that run from the fleshy substance of the muscle belly and insert into the particular bone they are going to move. They are most easily seen on the back of the hand where they stand out under the skin. Each individual muscle and its tendon form a 'muscle-tendon unit'.

Collagen is a relatively inelastic material made up of chains of proteins that varies little in its composition wherever it is found in the body. It is the principal material that makes up tendons and ligaments. It has a crimped structure that enables it to lengthen by about 10 per cent when subjected to load, but after this, if the force is too great, it tears.

Tendons are structurally very strong, but not indestructible. They have a much poorer blood supply than muscle and therefore have a lower metabolic rate. This means that they are capable of adaptation during training, but that this occurs at a much slower rate than in muscle. This can lead to problems in the early phases of a training programme (see Chapter 10). The poorer blood supply also means that they heal slowly after injury and are prone to develop overuse problems.

LIGAMENTS

Ligaments are structurally very similar to tendons, also being made up largely of collagen. All joints are surrounded by a fibrous capsule and the body uses ligaments as specialised static structures to provide extra stability. For example, there are small ligaments on either side of the finger joints to prevent sideways movements. The knee joint has a ligament on either side and another pair inside the knee to prevent excessive movement from front to back.

Ligaments are used by the body to both prevent abnormal movements and guide the normal movements of the joint and their integrity may be critical for normal function. Unfortunately, ligaments suffer from the same poor blood supply as the tendons and therefore are prone to the same healing problems.

3 Warming Up

When you start your car on a cold winter's morning it takes some time for the engine to get going and start performing efficiently. Your body is no different and to demand too much of it before it is ready is asking for trouble.

You will never see a top Olympic sprinter walk out on to the track, put on his spikes and get straight into the starting blocks. His warm up, for a nine-second race, will have started maybe an hour previously, slowly building up mentally and physically, so his mind and body are in the ideal state for the sound of the starting pistol.

If you visit your local climbing wall/crag, the situation is usually a little different. On with the tights, shoes and chalk bag and on to the wall/route. A large percentage of the injuries I see are associated with an inadequate warm up and demanding too much of the body before it is ready. Warming up should be an integral part of any training or climbing session and should come as automatically as putting on your boots or chalking up. The older and more decrepit you get, the more vital this becomes as your body slowly becomes less flexible and more reluctant to make the grand effort.

Because warming up is so important, this chapter is near the beginning of the book. Many aspects of training are incorporated in a warm up, so you will need to return to this chapter after absorbing the information in later chapters. Inevitably, some important points will be duplicated, but I hope this will help drive them home.

Warming up prepares the body for the increased demands you are going to place upon it. In one sense it literally 'warms up' the muscles, raising their temperature and improving the efficiency of the enzyme systems within the muscle cells that supply the energy needed for effort. It raises the heart and respiratory rates, increasing blood flow through the muscles and improving the delivery of oxygen and fuel to where it is most needed.

By warming up and stretching muscles, tendons and ligaments, you make them more pliable and decrease the risk of injury. By gradually increasing the demands made on the body, you don't suddenly subject it to a 'shock load' before it is ready. A proper warm up 'tunes in' the body, physically and mentally, by rehearsing the skills that are going to be required. Finally, a warm up should not be so intense as to leave you tired out but, after a short rest, raring to get on to the real challenge.

Cycling to the gym or climbing a wall, or humping a

Figures
1–5

pack up to the crag, are good ways to kick start the system. Otherwise, a bit of gentle jogging up and down, or a few minutes with a skipping rope or exercise bike will get the heart and lungs going and the blood circulating through the muscles. Then a bit of general loosening up with some arm circling, sideways bends, upright side to side twists, right hand to left ankle and vice versa (Figs 1–9).

Figures
6–9

Now you are ready for stretching. This is a very important part of a warm up and should be done before any type of training of climbing. This will not only help warm you up, but will keep you supple, decrease the chance of injury and prevent the tightening up of muscles that can occur if you are only concentrating on trying to gain strength. Move slowly into each stretch and hold for ten seconds. Stretch a little bit further and hold for another ten seconds. Relax and repeat. **Never bounce on a stretch.**

Run through a stretching routine as shown in Chapter 4.

At the same time as stretching, you can mentally warm up for the coming ordeal. Practice makes perfect, so do this every time and it will be easier in stressful situations. Relax as much as possible before each stretch and then focus your attention on the muscle group in question. Feel the muscle tense as the stretch is applied and then slowly relax as the seconds tick by. Inwardly repeat your favourite affirmations (see Chapter 7) to yourself while repeating the stretch.

Following the stretching sessions the next part of warming up is to tune in for the specific tasks ahead.

A good warming up exercise for climbers is to link your fingertips together and apply tension by trying to pull them apart. Holding the tension all the time, start with the arms above the head and move your arms slowly from one side to the other, over about thirty seconds. Then repeat at chest level and finally at waist level (Figs 10–15). Repeat the series again with your hands the other way round. At each level you will feel a different set of muscles come under tension. This exercise can even be used on small belay ledges!

For weight training, if following the traditional 3×10 RM (Repetition Maximum) sets routine, for each exercise do one set at 50 per cent of 10 RM (see Chapter 5) and one at 80 per cent of 10 RM, with a two-minute rest between each one before making the big effort.

Figures
10–15

17

For climbing, start with some easy pull-ups/circuits/routes on large holds. Following this, try a few problems of gradually increasing difficulty, to tune in the part of the nervous system responsible for placing parts of your body exactly where you want them. Try to be as precise as possible with your hands and feet.

At the end of this process you should feel warm, with the beginnings of a mild pump in your forearms. If using climbing or bouldering as training, start the hard work-out after a ten to fifteen-minute rest. Don't chill off in this period, put on another sweatshirt or fleece. If competing or red pointing, aim to leave fifteen to twenty minutes between finishing your physical warm up and climbing/competing. Keep well wrapped up, and gently repeat the loosening up exercises during this period to avoid cooling down too much. At a competition, if you have timed it right, this should see you through the holding area and to the front of the wall. This holding period is the time for final mental preparation, with relaxation, focusing, affirmation and visualisation (see Chapter 7).

WARMING DOWN

After a heavy session or hard route, warming down is important to help prevent muscle soreness. Repeat the loosening up exercises and the stretching routine after doing a few easy problems or series of exercises at a very light intensity. If this is followed by a long hot shower, it should see you ready for action the following day, without feeling as though you have been run over by a truck.

4   Flexibility

Few of us are inherently extremely flexible or 'double
jointed'. Those who are, often have one of a number of
inherited conditions in which the collagen that makes up
their tendons, ligaments and the tissue that surrounds the
joints is more elastic than in a normal person. This abnormal
flexibility can lead to a promising career as a circus con-
tortionist, but can also be a disadvantage in some situations,
making them prone to joint injuries.

If your structural make up is normal, then flexibility is
one of the things you can work at and achieve recognisable
improvements in a fairly short space of time. Stretching is
a natural activity (watch your cat or dog) and there is a
good deal of evidence from the field of sports medicine that
problems such as tendinitis often start when muscles and
tendons are too stiff and inflexible. This becomes more
noticeable and more difficult to change as you get older.
Females tend to be more naturally flexible than males but
for both sexes, the younger you start, the easier it will be
to maintain good flexibility.

Stretching can be done at home, on your own, and
requires no specialised equipment. It can be done while
reading, listening to music, or watching the TV or your
favourite climbing video. I have seen it said in print that
'stretching is boring'. It is true that it is not the most exciting
activity in the world, but you can combine it with rehearsing
some of your mental skills, thus killing two birds with one
stone.

Is it worth it? Does flexibility help you to climb? When
first taught to climb, the golden rule is to keep your body
away from the rock and your weight over your feet. As
climbs get increasingly vertical, however, it becomes more
and more important to be able to get your body closer and
closer to the rock. This avoids having your rear end sticking
out into space, taking your centre of gravity out behind
your feet, and therefore putting more strain on your already
pumped arms. To get your weight over your feet on steep
rock requires good flexibility in turning out your hip joints.

Flexibility around the hip joints is also important in heel hooking and in situations where you need to reach that wide bridge or get your foot up enough for that high step up on to a handhold. If you lack flexibility, it means finding a less efficient way to do a move or risking an agonising twang when pushing your tendons and ligaments just that bit too far.

Injury tends to occur at the point when a muscle/tendon unit is already stretched to its limit. When it is as tight as a bowstring, it takes very little extra to produce a tear. If you can increase the range in which a muscle tendon unit can work comfortably, then you can decrease the chance of injuring yourself.

In your arms, suppleness of your forearm muscles helps prevent you being sidelined with 'tennis' or 'golfer's' elbow. Flexibility around the shoulder joint helps prevent injury. Stretching your fingers helps prevent the development of deformity in the joints.

Stretching should be an integral part of any training programme for improving your climbing. It will enable you to improve your technique by making you less dependent on strength and power. It is a mistake to ignore this facet of training in preference for the manic development of muscle.

Although stretching does increase the metabolic rate of muscles and tendons, it is *not* a substitute for a proper warm up. It should, however, be an integral part of your warming up ritual.

TYPES OF STRETCH

Ballistic Stretching

I will briefly mention this in order to immediately dismiss it. It was thought, at one time, that by stretching a muscle and then bouncing on it you could produce the desired effect. Muscles and tendons possess specialised nerve endings which are sensitive to being stretched, and tell the body that the muscle/tendon is being pulled apart. The body then reacts by contracting the affected muscle to oppose the stretching action.

By bouncing on a stretch, you activate these receptors and actually produce the opposite effect to the one you are trying to achieve. It can also produce injury. NEVER bounce on a stretch.

Static Stretching

By slowly applying a stretch, you avoid activating these stretch receptors. The technique is to slowly apply a stretch until the muscle/tendon feels tight and then hold it for ten seconds. During this time period there will be some relaxation of the tissues and so you can then stretch a little bit further until the muscle/tendon is tight again, and then hold it for another ten seconds. Then relax completely and start again. Usually one goes through three cycles before moving on to a different stretch. Do not push your muscles past the point of feeling tight and tear them. Stretching should not be painful and the 'no pain no gain' cliché does not apply in this situation!

Proprioceptive Neuromuscular Facilitation

This technique is based on the fact that after a maximal muscular contraction maximal relaxation occurs. In order to practise it you need a partner you trust implicitly as, applied wrongly, it is easy to produce injury.

Figure 1   If applied to an adductor stretch (Fig 1), the knees are

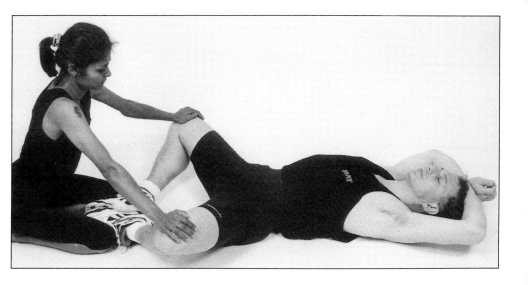

initially held in the position of maximal stretch. Then, held in this position, you try and bring your knees together as hard as you can against the resistance of your partner for a period of six seconds. Then relax and your partner gently presses your knees apart again, as far as they will go, until your adductor muscles become tight again. The cycle is repeated three times for each type of stretch.

Now you know the theory, I will run through a series of stretches appropriate to climbing that will help you become more flexible and decrease your chances of injury or of developing tendinitis. Few people reading this will be able to achieve extreme positions straight away. Take it sensibly, slowly working into each stretch to the point of tension and holding it. As the weeks go by you will improve, providing you practise regularly!

Figures
2–3

Lower Limb Stretches

Calf Stretches (Figs 2, 3): While standing, keep your heel flat on the floor and lean forward until you feel the tension in your calf. Hold it for ten seconds, then, keeping your heel flat on the ground, bend your knee and you will feel a different muscle stretch. Hold again for ten seconds and relax.

Quadriceps Stretch (Fig 4): Grasp your ankle in your hand and pull your heel up towards your buttocks. Lean slightly forward to keep your balance.

Figure 4

Hamstring Stretches (Figs 5, 6): Often very tight in men. You can do these one of several ways. Sitting, bend the other leg up at the knee. Then, keeping your leg flat on the floor, slide your hands down your leg, aiming to grasp your ankle and put your head on your knees. Standing, use the stair bannister or any flat surface of a convenient height. Put your heel up on the top and again lean forward, aiming to hold your ankle and put your head on your knees.

Figures
5–6

Flexibility

Pyriformis Stretch (Fig 7): While sitting, bend up one leg and then place its foot on the other side of the opposite leg, at the level of the knee. Apply a stretch using your arm on the same side.

Figure 7

25

Adductor Stretches (Figs 8–10): Probably one of the most useful stretches and another area that is particularly inflexible in many men. When you are beginning, use the stretch lying down with your ankles together. As you improve, you can apply a gentle pressure by putting a small weight on your knees. When you become good at this, add the stretch up against a wall. Again, you can increase the pressure by attaching a small weight to each ankle. In both cases always keep your lumbar spine supported with a pillow in the small of your back.

Figures
8–10

Trunk and Spine Stretches

Side Trunk Stretch (Fig 11): While standing, stretch one leg sideways until the other leg is bent at a right angle. Lean down sideways towards the bent leg and put your hand on the floor behind your foot. Stretch the other arm across and over your head, and lean further until you feel the stretch up the side of your body.

Figure 11

Spine Stretch: Lie face down. Put your hands at the level of your shoulders and slowly lift your head and shoulders up and back, keeping your pelvis in contact with the floor.

Spine twist (Fig 12): Sit on the floor. Bring one knee up and put the hand on the same side behind you. Using the opposite arm to assist, turn away and back, twisting your spine until you feel the tension.

Figure 12

Upper Limb Stretches

Posterior Shoulder and Latissimus Stretch (Fig 13): Lift your arm up and place your hand between your shoulder blades. Using the other hand, pull gently on the elbow until you reach sufficient tension.

Figures
13–15

Posterior Shoulder and Triceps Stretch (Fig 14): Put your arm across in front of your body and, using the opposite forearm, apply the stretch.

Anterior Shoulder Stretch (Fig 15): This is more easily performed with a partner (you can trust!) but a door frame or vertical edge of any sort can be used.

Forearm Flexor Stretch (Figs 16, 17): Can be done using the floor or a table top, or by bending the wrist back with the other hand.

Forearm Extensor Stretch (Figs 18, 19): This is done the same way as the forearm flexor stretch, but obviously the hand is stretched in the opposite direction.

Figures
16–17

This sounds like a huge list of exercises but, once you get

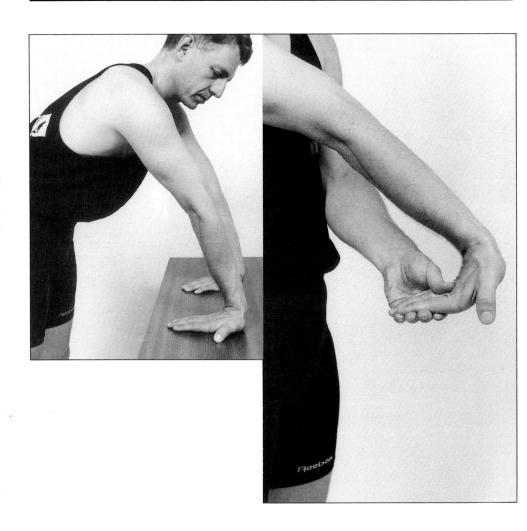

into the swing of things, it can be carried out fairly quickly. At twenty seconds a stretch, repeated three times, the whole lot should take about fifteen minutes. Remember that stretching is a relaxed activity and cannot be rushed – take it gently. If you are inflexible to start with, three sessions a week should produce fairly rapid improvements. If you think this time will be difficult to find, these sessions can be carried out as part of an extended warm up for climbing or weight training.

Figures
18–19

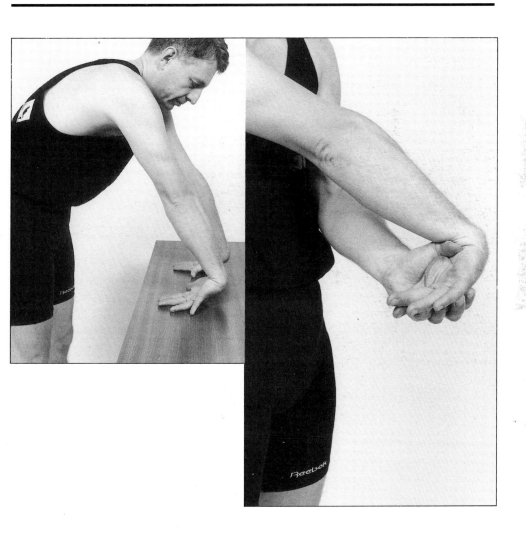

5   In the Gym

Why train in the gym? I have often heard climbers saying that 'the best form of training for climbers is climbing'. To a certain extent this is true. No matter how much sweat you shed pulling weights, if you never touch rock you are unlikely to become an elite climber. Climbing and bouldering are excellent training for developing the skills of climbing, for putting together the strength, balance and agility to produce that more or less graceful movement up the rockface.

However, if you want to make gains in muscle and tendon strength and endurance, to both improve performance and help prevent injury, in a way that is both controllable and easily monitored, working with weights (this includes your own bodyweight) in the gym or at home is the way to go. **It is very important, however, that the exercises imitate climbing movements as closely as possible,** otherwise you will just become good at pulling weights. Think about the position of your hands and arms in each exercise and change them as appropriate.

In Chapter 1 I mentioned the basic principle of progressive overload. This means that, in order to keep gaining in strength and endurance, one has to keep increasing the loads or number of repetitions, and exercising to the point of muscle failure. Muscle failure is that agonising point where the muscles are burning and you just can't perform one more repetition. A partner is really useful here, to ensure that you don't drop a great weight on your head or across your chest. It does not mean you attempt to pick up a weight that is obviously too great, and tear a muscle in half.

This is why it is difficult to get the same improvements with bouldering or at the crag, as it would often be dangerous to push yourself to the point where your muscles fail (unless you are top roping) and you can't control the situation in which they do fail. Other advantages of gym work are that you can work on specific muscles in isolation and can closely monitor improvement by keeping a log of the number of repetitions, maximal load lifted etc. By controlling the application of load, one avoids the shock loading that can occur when grabbing at a hold, or a foot slipping off, suddenly putting all your weight on that one finger in a pocket, which often results in injury. By specifically improving the strength of the muscles used in climbing you decrease the chance of injury at the crag, by bringing even those moves which require great strength or power within the working range of your muscles. All this can be carried out in the muggy warmth of the gym when it is dark, cold, snowing or pouring with rain outside.

STRENGTH, POWER AND ENDURANCE

As explained in Chapter 2, the extent to which you can develop any of these specific characteristics of muscle function may well be genetically determined. You can, however, make the most of the genetic hand you've been dealt.

Anyone who has worked out in a gym knows that, initially, gains in strength are reasonably easy to make using the principle of progressive overload. Power is defined as force divided by time and so produces that explosion of strength needed in dynoing for that distant hold. Endurance is the ability to keep going, and for many of us is the critical factor while climbing, when our grossly pumped forearms cannot control the slow uncurling of our fingers from relatively good holds. Each of these aspects of muscle function can be specifically trained for, and you can tailor your training programme to improve any deficiencies that may exist in your climbing ability.

One of the major worries of many climbers is that weight training will cause them to bulk out and become like the grotesque 'Michelin Man' seen on the front of bodybuilding magazines. This does not usually happen if you are careful about avoiding anabolic steroids and if you structure your programme for climbing, and it has been shown that most people can make significant gains in strength without increasing muscle bulk. This is particularly so for women.

In simple terms, strength is gained by lifting large loads for a small number of repetitions, whereas endurance is gained by lifting lighter loads for a large number of repetitions. Trying to gain in power should be reserved until significant gains in strength have been achieved, otherwise you will overload the relevant muscles and injure yourself.

Training for strength begins by finding your repetition maximum (RM) for any given exercise. This is the weight you can just lift for ten repetitions. This will obviously change as your training programme progresses. When you can lift your original RM for fifteen repetitions, it is time to increase the load and train with your new '10 RM'.

Traditional weight training programmes use three sets of 10 RM for any given exercise with a rest of two minutes between each set. Always start with one set at half your RM and one at 80 per cent before going on to the proper sets. Repetitions should be carried out smoothly, and breathing should be regular, with an inhalation and exhalation during each repetition. It is very tempting to take a deep breath in and hold it as you exert yourself, but this is a bad technique and can result in wild fluctuations in blood pressure.

Training for power is along the same lines but make each movement as explosive as possible. I repeat, do not try to make gains in power before having made steady gains in strength.

Training to improve the endurance of an individual muscle group involves using large numbers of repetitions with loads of about 70 per cent RM. Keep going until the muscles you are working on develop the slow burning sensation most climbers will recognise, having experienced

Figure 1
The Weight Training Pyramid

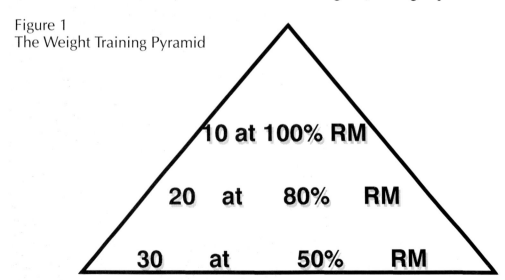

10 at 100% RM

20 at 80% RM

30 at 50% RM

pumped forearms. This means you are pushing the relevant muscles beyond their capacity to keep working aerobically.

While traditional weight training regimes for gaining strength work on the three sets of 10 RM principle, I think there is much to be gained by climbers using a 'pyramidal' approach to each exercise. By staring with a low load/high repetition set and building up to a high load/low repetition set, one can produce gains both in strength and endurance. This also means that, by the time you start reaching maximum effort, you are well warmed up and are therefore less likely to injure yourself. The plan for this approach is seen opposite in Fig 1.

Back Extensions and Abdominal Curls

A strong back and abdomen provide the platform for the

Figure 2

upper body to work on and it is a mistake to ignore these two areas. With back extensions, start with three sets of ten, and over the weeks slowly work up to three sets of thirty. Likewise with abdominal curls. To make these more difficult you can gradually increase the slope of the exercise bench (Fig 2).

Lat Pull Downs (Figs 3–5)

The latissimus dorsi is the so called 'climbing muscle' and is the major muscle used when pulling up. Vary the position of your hands on the bar and, instead of using a whole hand grip, use just your fingers. Pull the bar down to your chest and lock off, then return to the start position slowly. Work on muscles used for pulling up on undercuts by holding the bar with your palms towards you. You can use a set of 50 per cent RM as a warming up exercise, prior to doing pull ups.

Figures 3–5

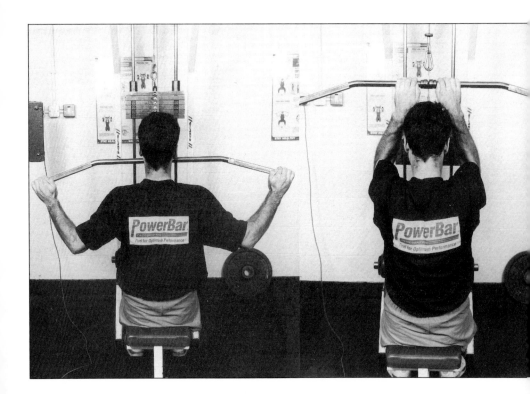

Pull Ups

The traditional pull up is an exercise that is favoured by
many climbers. Even here, performing the exercise in the
right way can improve the outcome. I would suggest the
following routine: After warming up, start with a set of five
pull ups. After a short rest, start by hanging from a full
stretch, pull up and lock off. Swing your right foot up to
touch the bar on the right, lower it and then swing your
left foot up to touch the bar on the left (Figs 6–7). *Lower
slowly* to a full-arm stretch and repeat. Avoid hanging for
long periods at a full stretch, as it can cause shoulder injury.
Aim for three sets of ten with a two-minute rest between
each one. If you can't manage a set of ten to start with, do
as many as you can, with your partner giving you a bit of
help for the last desperate pull up at the point of failure.
Vary the distance between your hands with each set. When
you can do three sets comfortably, at the next sessions add
a five-pound weight round your waist and start again. Once

you have gained strength, you can work on power by making each pull up explosively fast. You can work on endurance by increasing the number of repetitions.

When you get really good, you can try pull ups with one arm, with the same sequence of pull up, lock off and lower slowly. It may be helpful at this stage to give yourself a little help by using some bungi cord to take a little of your weight (Fig 1, p. 51).

Figures
6–7

Seated Cable Rows

This exercise helps to prepare you for those powerful under-cuts and to work on the muscles that help stabilise the shoulder blades. Change the usual handles for a short bar that you can grip with your fingers as if holding on to an undercut. Power in these situations is usually not as import-ant as strength, so do the exercise at a steady pace. Pull in to the waist, making sure the shoulders are fully braced back (Fig 8). Lock off and then let out the weight slowly and under control, concentrating on keeping the shoulder blades well braced back.

Figure 8

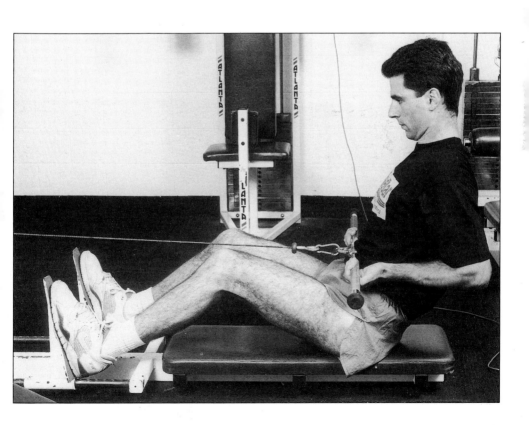

Flyes (Figs 9–10)

These work your chest, shoulders and upper-back muscles, and are performed with free weights while lying on a bench. They should be performed both lying on your back and lying on your front, to balance the muscles at the front and back of your shoulders. Keep your elbows slightly bent and make the movement occur at your shoulders.

Figures
9–10

Bench Press (Fig 11)

This exercise is effectively a press up lying on your back. It works both your triceps and your chest muscles. Follow the standard weight routine as described above. Alter weight/reps/speed to suit your requirements. Only work to failure if you have a partner who can help on the last rep.

Figure 11

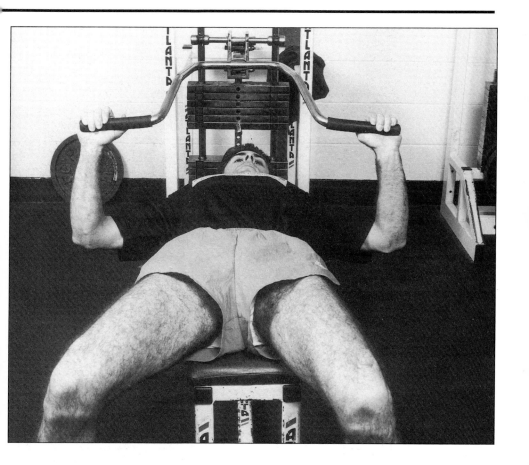

Lateral Raises and Pull Downs

These exercises can be done using a special piece of apparatus called a cable crossover machine. If your gym does not have one of these, the exercises can be done with an old bicycle inner tube, or a 'theraband', as described on page

84–5, where they are described for use in shoulder rehabilitation. The key part of this exercise is to keep your shoulder
blade as steady as possible. When first starting, do the
exercise one arm at a time and feel the point of the shoulder
blade with the other hand. Aim to keep it as still as you
can, as you either pull your arm down across your body or
pull it across, up and away.

Dips (Figs 12–13)

These work the triceps. This is useful when pushing down
on to holds and also helps balance the muscles around the
shoulder. Start with the standard three sets of ten. Vary
your hands from thumb forwards to thumb backwards for

Figures
12–13

each set. Once this becomes easy, start adding weight to your waist. If you want to improve endurance, increase the number of reps.

Leg Exercises

Huge, muscular legs are generally not very important to climbers. You can work your calves on the edge of a step, aiming for endurance rather than power, by having a weight on your shoulders and then holding the position for as long as possible.

Train for high rockovers, using anything stable that you can get your foot up on to. Steady yourself with your hands and sink as low as possible before getting your weight up on to your foot and standing up. Five reps for each leg should be sufficient.

If you get bored with these exercises, most gyms will have staff who will be able to tell you different methods of working the same muscles. Always try and relate the way you do each exercise to climbing and try to see in what situations the strength of a particular muscle group may be of benefit.

6 Bouldering, Climbing and Climbing Walls

Climbing in some form is, without doubt, the best way of improving your technique. If you watch any top climber at a competition or on a hard red point, it is the smoothest and most stylish climbers that tend to do well. Good technique, with precise footwork and the ability to instinctively use holds to their best advantage, leads to an economy of effort, making the best of any endurance, strength and flexibility that you have worked so hard to develop.

During the hours spent practising climbing, train your brain to automatically recognise when a handhold or foothold is within reach and how to use it. The more you climb, the more likely any new sequence of moves will be similar to something you have met before. These factors enable your climbing on the crag to become more fluent, and help you to flow up the rock rather than stutter from hold to hold.

Work on your weaknesses and improve your strengths. Work on techniques for improving reach and keeping in balance on steep rock, such as the 'knee drop' (on a high foothold, outside edge with the foot and bend the knee down and in), and learn to deadpoint and dyno in low-level safety. The flat nature of many panel walls, associated with the projecting nature of the holds, means that techniques learned only on artificial walls may not be applicable on the crag, but as long as you are aware of this it shouldn't be a problem.

To become good at on-sighting requires regular practice at on-sighting, not just endlessly dogging routes at the crag or wall! Learn to mentally work through a route when looking at it from below. Look for potential rests, and then try and visualise the sequences between them. Learn to use each rest to the full, relaxing as much as possible and breathing deeply and slowly, and then try and climb steadily between rests without stopping, except to clip gear. On easy routes at the wall or crag, a good way to improve your technique is to commit yourself to using every hold you touch. This makes you think before you move and also makes you explore the different ways any individual hold may be used.

Climbing and bouldering can also be used to develop finger strength and endurance as well as general arm strength and power. The advent of top-roped leading walls has probably been the biggest advance in enabling you to use climbing for training, but to make the most of them you need to approach your training in a structured and disciplined way.

CLIMBING WALLS

Whatever grade you are climbing, you can use a leading, or any reasonable wall, to improve your strength and endurance. Top ropes, however, certainly make pushing yourself to the point of failure somewhat safer!

Try this routine – pick three routes you know reasonably well, one at just below the hardest grade you are climbing, one two or three grades below this, and the third two or three grades below this again. After warming up properly, climb the easiest route at a reasonable speed then climb down *slowly*. Concentrate on climbing as beautifully as you can – precise footwork, hit the handholds just right first time, and learn to use just enough strength to keep you there. Without resting, power up the route, then climb down slowly again. Always aim to come down under control – *never* drop on to a hand hold. If climbing up involved a large dyno, or you are just too pumped, get your belayer to take some of the strain as you come down.

Take two minutes' rest, and repeat the whole sequence for the middle-grade route. Take another two minutes' rest and then repeat for the hardest route. Rest for five minutes and repeat the sequence for the middle route. Rest for two minutes and then finish off on the easiest route again. If at any point you become totally pumped, lower off, take a fifteen-minute rest and start at the easiest route again. Keep going to the point of failure, always warming down on an easy route before finishing. The aim should be to complete the session by only just being able to complete the easiest route.

When you can do the whole routine without getting too pumped, increase the difficulty of the routes. If you are trying to develop your strength, you can do this routine with a weight belt. Use easier grades and gradually increase the weight as you get stronger, always aiming to reach the point of muscle failure at some point during the routine. If you feel you are strong enough but want to develop arm power, use a weight belt but aim to explode up the routes, making the moves as dynamic as possible. If it's finger power you are after, use routes with smaller holds, but move smoothly from hold to hold – don't make sudden grabs for small holds while wearing a weight belt, it's a good way to injure yourself. This sort of routine can be adapted to suit whatever your needs might be.

Going up and down is preferable to going round and round, but if your local wall cannot be adapted for top-roped climbing, there are still ways it can be used to improve your performance. The confidence with which you then approach vertical training on this type of wall is probably proportional to the thickness of the crash mats!

Traversing is certainly not as much fun as lead climbing and, unless you are into doing a lot of girdles, is not as immediately applicable to the crag. It is, however, a reasonable way of improving finger endurance. To preserve your finger joints, where possible, traverse on holds which are no narrower than the end joint of your fingers and, to preserve your limbs, at a height where it is reasonably safe to fall off. The aim is to keep going until your fingers start to uncurl from even quite large holds. Imitate climbing by finding rests on the wall and shaking out. When you can't go on any further, rest for fifteen minutes, then traverse again until really pumped. Rest for a further fifteen minutes and go for a final pumped session, using your mental grit to keep you on the wall, even though your forearms are about to explode! It is easy to monitor improvement by keeping a record of how far you can go each time before failing.

If you want to develop arm strength, use routes or circuits with reasonably sized handholds, without using any footholds. Overhanging walls with large holds are ideal for this, with preferably five or six consecutive dynos. I believe it is better not to downclimb in this mode as the sudden dropping on to the next hold down can lead to shoulder injury. Keep going until your arms are burning, then rest for ten minutes and repeat. Have another rest and go for a final arm blast. When you become good at this, add a weight belt.

Always finish any session at a wall with ten minutes of warming down, doing some easy problems or traversing, following by loosening-up exercises and some gentle stretching.

Many climbers now create their own mini walls in their own homes and cellars with plywood panels and bolt on holds. You can play at designing hard problems to improve any aspect of your climbing, or tailor the moves to simulate the cruxes of routes you are having difficulty with. It is useful to incorporate a couple of easy problems, a traverse on large holds, or a fingerboard, to warm up on.

CLIMBING AND BOULDERING

Many of our top climbers regard bouldering as one of the best ways of developing technique and power. As with any other sort of training, to use boulders to give you the maximum benefit requires a carefully calculated approach. Working with a partner is very useful, to both provide encouragement and support, and to make landing safer in the event of coming off.

You need to develop a circuit of problems, starting at the straightforward ones and working slowly up to those you find very hard. Also pick out some that are currently beyond your ability. Warm up properly and perform each problem twice, as usual concentrating on performing them as gracefully and effortlessly as possible. Experiment with the way you grip the holds and explore the best ways of keeping as much weight on your feet as possible. Rest for two minutes between each problem. Once you are on to the hard problems, repeat them in sequence until really pumped, and then work your way back down the grades, finishing on the easy problems. When you have improved to the point where you can cruise what were once really hard problems, start trying the problems that were out of reach.

Bouldering, like using climbing walls, can be tailored to your individual requirements. If it is finger strength you want, start your circuit with problems with reasonable sized holds and pick successive problems with smaller and smaller holds. If it is arm strength you lack, pick steeper and steeper problems and all the overhangs you can find. For power, find problems that require dynamic moves from more and more tenuous positions. If you want to improve any of these beyond that which you can achieve with your own body, wear a weight belt, starting at around 2–3Kg. and building slowly up to about 7.5Kg. This is particularly relevant to those of us who still climb with a full rack! Be careful, as uncontrolled moves can easily injure your fingers. Falls are much more difficult to control and are much harder on your knees and ankles while wearing extra weight – pick your landings with care!

Using actual routes for training can be much riskier. You can either keep soloing routes well within your capabilities until starting to get pumped (I don't think this is a particularly good way of trying to improve, as you can't, with any safety, push at your limits), or set up top ropes on harder routes and repeatedly climb them up *and* down (under control) until you reach the point of failure. Rest for ten minutes and then repeat the routine the same way again, or use the time to set up a top rope on another climb. This does tend to get rather tedious for both climber and belayer, and, unless at an unpopular crag, annoy other people trying to get on to the routes.

FINGERBOARDS

For many of us without the space or the finances a finger-board is about as close to climbing at home as we get. There is quite a variety of these available and all you need to ensure is that there is a range of holds, from jugs to small crimps, on which to practise. Regular training on a fingerboard can increase finger and upper-limb strength and endurance, but does tend to get rather tedious after the initial burst of enthusiasm has faded. The great thing about fingerboards is that the stress and strain you put your fingers through is under control and you therefore reduce the risk of injury. It is better to work smoothly and statically rather than trying to move your weight around the board from small edge to small edge. Long deadhangs from small edges are not recommended, as they increase the chances of joint injury.

When starting on small holds or progressing on to one-arm work, the use of one or two $\frac{1}{4}$- or $\frac{1}{2}$-inch bungi cords, to take some of the strain from a fully locked off position to full stretch, can be very helpful (Fig 1). Some people find it preferable to clip these into a harness, as when using them for your feet, a slip can result in a smarting smack in the face!

Figure 1

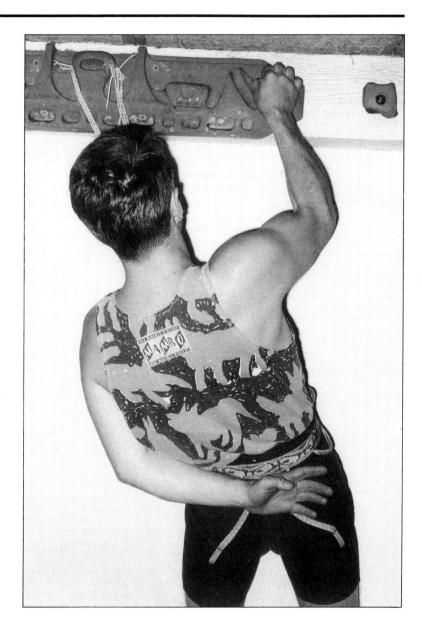

Pyramids of pull ups or lock offs (in various degrees of arm bend), can be performed, working from big holds down to small holds and then back again. You can either use counting seconds or the number of repetitions as the basis for each set, e.g. after warming up, twenty pull ups on large holds – *thirty seconds rest*; fifteen pull ups on moderate holds – *twenty seconds rest*; ten pull ups on small holds – *fifteen seconds rest*; fifteen pull ups on moderate holds – *thirty seconds rest*; twenty pull ups on large holds. The aim should be to get very pumped and only just be able to complete the last set. When first starting, you can reduce the numbers of repetitions or use the help of some bungi cords. If you are not getting pumped at the end of the last set, increase the number of repetitions in each set or use three sets of smaller holds. When you really improve, aim to do three complete pyramids with a ten to fifteen-minute break between each pyramid.

Once you are happy with your two-arm strength and want to work on one-arm pull ups, use bungi cords that will take enough of your weight to allow you to complete one pull up. Either clip them to your harness or grip them in the opposite hand. If you are having difficulty initiating a pull up, start from a locked off position and slowly lower under control. Rest and repeat until no longer able to control the movement. Repeat this sequence at least three times a week, slowly decreasing the support from the bungis as you gain in strength.

7   Mind Training

We all know the feeling – as the crux approaches, the pulse quickens, your hands sweat and rising doubts cloud the mind, 'Am I good enough? Will I fall and my last runner pop, leaving me a screaming portion of crag pizza on the ground below?'

So, instead of climbing with your usual smooth and unhurried style, an undignified scrabbling carries you through to easier ground and the realisation that it wasn't nearly as hard as you had mentally built it up to be. Even worse, a problem that you would cruise at the wall or on a boulder, completely defeats you when sixty feet up and thirty feet above your last poor RP, leaving you feeling an inadequate, miserable specimen of a human being and sending you skulking home to kick the dog.

Some people are born with no sense of fear and either go on to great things or an early grave. For most of us mere mortals, however, controlling anxiety can be a real problem. All is not lost, though, as anxiety control is just one of a number of mental skills that can be acquired using suitable training techniques. For many climbers at any grade, mental skills may be the most important facet of climbing training, as so often it is the ability to focus your concentration, dismiss distractions and quell anxiety that is the fine line between the buzz of success in your head, or the whistle of the wind in your ears as you gain a bit more air time!

In these competition days, proper mental preparation can make the difference between the winner's rostrum or depressing failure, and may be the critical factor at the top level. If less than totally confident, it can be easy to get yourself into a downward spiral of negative thoughts, leaving you in the immediate pre-climb holding area, clammy, miserable and wondering 'what on earth am I doing here?', already having defeated yourself before even touching the wall!

As in any other sort of training there are no easy short cuts. Mental training will not teach you to levitate, or magically enable you to become world champion, but it will help you to make sure that the sacrifices you have made, and the sweat you have shed in the other parts of your training programme, will not be wasted.

Just as there are a wide variety of body types which respond to different sorts of physical training in different ways, so the way in which each individual's brain responds to stimuli may also be quite varied. Broadly speaking, people are said to divide into two main groups, with the 'Aristotelians' being more obsessed with detail and order, and the 'Platoists' liking more broad and sweeping thought processes. Most of us have the ability to shift, to a certain extent, from one mode to the other, but there is usually a preferred way of thinking. This will have some influence on the way you approach the variety of available techniques. Within this broad subdivision, individuals will respond best to different types of stimuli, e.g. sound or vision.

In this chapter I will outline a number of techniques that have been tried and tested in other sports, and which are applicable in rock climbing. There are a vast array of techniques to choose from, none of which are likely to be a universal panacea. You will have to try them out and see which techniques prove to be the most powerful for you.

Step one in planning any programme is to set yourself some goals, thinking hard about what it is you are aiming for. What is it you ultimately want to achieve? This might be anything from 'To climb Flying Buttress at Stanage', to 'My goal is to be sport climbing champion of the world'.

It is important to be realistic, however, and there are some criteria which your goals should fulfil. They should neither be too hard nor too easy. The first will ultimately lead to disappointment and therefore a lowering in confidence, while the second will leave you dissatisfied and knowing inside that you have 'cheated' yourself.

Try not to be too nebulous (i.e. 'my goal is to be a better climber') or you will be left not knowing exactly what you are aiming for, resulting in unstructured preparation. Your goals should not be subject to outside influence, leaving you feeling out of control, and it is better if there is some way of actually measuring your progress.

Once you have decided on your ultimate goal, write it down on a piece of paper. Now decide roughly how long this is liable to take you, or how long you are willing to dedicate to this aim. Olympic athletes generally have a four-year plan, aiming to peak at the right time, or if a young athlete, it may even be the Olympics after next. They will have a defined series of times to achieve by certain dates, and a series of intermittent competitions to work up for in the interim. Once you have decided on a time scale, try and think of some intermediate goals that you will have to achieve along the way and a rough estimate of when you want to achieve these.

What you will then have is a series of steps going from 'what I want to achieve this month' (which may be to climb a particular route or problem) to 'what I want to achieve this season', and then to 'what I want to achieve in a year's time' etc., all of which gradually lead you to your ultimate goal.

Once you have a rough plan, write down some active measures which will help you reach your goal in a month's time ('I will stick to my training schedule', 'I will manage an extra five pull ups', 'I will lose 4Kg. in weight' etc.). Obviously these active measures will need upgrading as you go along. By subdividing your goals into small, realistic and attainable steps, you can keep your motivation going by being able to see steady progress and reaffirming your belief in yourself as a wonderful human being.

As man has evolved, the body has developed mechanisms for providing that bit extra in desperate or dangerous situations, the so called 'fight or flight' response. A large surge of adrenaline is released, accelerating the heart rate, increasing the depth of breathing and heightening the responsiveness of the nervous system. These effects can be useful when approaching the crux, but some of the associated effects, such as sweating, the shakes, and an intense desire to empty your bowels or bladder, may be somewhat less beneficial.

We all know that good climbing performances usually occur when we are most relaxed and confident, and bad ones when we are tense and distracted. The skill is in being able to attain the right frame of mind when everything is working against you.

The first step in most mental exercises is to *relax*. You may say that any fool can relax – eight pints of beer does the trick for most of us! In reality, relaxing so you are alert while the mind is calm and empty is not quite so easy. If you close your eyes and try and empty your mind, to let it go blank and think about nothing, stray thoughts tend to crop up, and your mind will wander off down all sorts of odd alleyways. What you will be trying to achieve with training, is the ability to still your mind and reach a state where you are both focused and relaxed at the same time.

Being able to achieve this state is desirable before any sort of mental exercise, and may even help you live longer! You don't need joss sticks, prayer bells and mantras, or even to contort yourself into the lotus position to achieve it, although some people find these adjuncts a help. Practising this art is best done after a training session, and before rather than after a meal. Relaxation can be used when warming up or down, to help you calm down before climbing a hard route or in a competition, and before any form of visualisation.

A simple technique, practised in yoga for centuries, is to concentrate on your breathing. Make sure you are sitting comfortably and unlikely to be interrupted. Close your eyes and breathe in slowly through your nose. Feel the air as it enters and follow it mentally as it travels down into your lungs, and then, as you breathe out, slowly follow it back out again. Don't try too hard, the whole process should be as effortless as possible. If stray thoughts interrupt, acknowledge them and then gently bring your mind back to concentrating on your breathing again.

Some people find it easier to silently count at the end of each breath, up to ten then start again at one. Using this method requires a mixture of relaxation and concentration at the same time. You should practise either of these breathing techniques for at least five minutes every day. You should find that, if done regularly, you will be able to reach the state of relaxed awareness with less and less difficulty and with fewer and fewer mental interruptions.

Another useful technique is 'progressive muscular relaxation'. Lie down somewhere comfortable and relax for a couple of minutes. Now focus on your feet and scrunch up your toes as hard as you can. Mentally identify and focus on the muscles that are working. Hold the tension for about fifteen seconds and then relax. Mentally scan the muscles that are now relaxed and be aware of the different feeling in them between being tense and their now relaxed state.

Gradually work up your body, repeating the process of tensing and relaxing for your calves, the muscles on the front of your shins, the muscles on the front of your thighs and your hamstrings, in turn. Repeat the process for your arms, starting with making as tight a fist as possible and working up through your biceps and triceps to your shoulders. Then your stomach and back muscles, finishing with your neck and finally your facial muscles. This whole process should take about fifteen minutes and, to become good at it, needs to be practised every day.

Once you have mastered this technique, you can use it while climbing! Not by lying down and becoming comatose at the foot of the crag, but as a technique for identifying groups of muscles that are inappropriately or over tensed, and then relaxing them. With practice this can be performed in a matter of a few seconds. Try it on the wall or on an extended boulder problem. When approaching a difficult section, hold it for a moment and mentally check for muscle groups that are unnecessarily tense and relax them. It may be you are overgripping with your fingers – learn the amount of force you need to apply to just hold on without wasting energy. It may be your shoulders are tense or your face may be clenched in a rigid mask of fear!

Anxiety can sometimes be handled by reducing it into manageable portions. If you look up at a route and are totally phased, look at the first section up to where you can clip the first bolt or place your first runner. If you can handle this, work out your tactics for the next section to a rest, and then set off. This strategy may not be advisable on a chop route, unless you are absolutely determined to have a go!

When fear becomes overwhelming, you've mentally said goodbye to the world and are ready to give up and fall off, you need some way of regaining control. A technique that comes from the world of martial arts (particularly *aikido*) is *centring*. Stand with your eyes closed and relax for a couple of minutes. Then take a deep breath in and focus your attention in the middle of your forehead. As you breath slowly out, feel this focus move (and mentally direct it) slowly down your body to a point just below your navel (this point corresponds to the centre of gravity of your body). You should feel relaxed and in balance. Hold this sensation and focus of attention for as long as possible.

When you can accomplish this with ease, open your eyes and try walking around with your focus of attention still held at this point. You should find you move with more grace and balance than usual.

With practice, this technique can be perfected to the point where just by breathing in and concentrating on your centre of gravity you can instantly refocus, putting yourself 'in balance'. If you add a positive statement such as 'I am excited by this' (rather than 'I am scared by this' – fear and excitement produce very similar physiological effects on the body), and smile, this may see you through some sticky situations. Centring can also be used in any situation which requires you to quickly refocus your attention, and is as useful at the start of a route as for steadying yourself before launching up for the crux or that distant dyno.

Concentration is the focusing of the mind on the here and now – not on what has just happened or will happen, but on this immediate moment. To achieve this one must learn to cope with distractions and to dissociate oneself from them. These may be anything from that annoying prat at the foot of the crag trying to tell you how to do the route, or noticing your last runner has lifted out, to the fear you are going to fall off the crux and deck it, or even the appreciative 'oohs' and 'ahs' of the crowd as they thrill to your graceful movements up the wall.

Concentration should be relaxed and not strained and, when practised well, will block out your worries and fears and help you reach the so-called 'peak performance state' – totally absorbed in the here and now and able to react instantly with maximum effectiveness. Watch an Olympic long jumper prepare for his jump, working himself up, then focusing on the runway and becoming totally immune to the noise of the crowd, the cameramen etc. and totally absorbed with the job he has to do. For a climber it means, as each move or sequence of moves is made, it is dismissed and your attention should be brought back to the immediate moment. It is no good thinking that the crux looks hard when it is many moves away, you are likely to make a mistake before you get there. Equally, having completed a very hard move, don't dwell on it but concentrate on the move you are now making – save your celebrations for the top.

If problems at home with your partner, work or previous failure are interfering with your ability to focus on the job at hand, a commonly employed method for dealing with them is the 'black box' technique. Close your eyes and relax. Then imagine yourself sitting at a table with pen and paper. On the desk is a black box with a slot in the top. Imagine writing down a word or phrase that sums up your present worries on the paper then folding it up and putting it through the slot into the box. As you put the paper into the box you must be aware that the problem has been set aside for the present, allowing you to concentrate on your current task. You must make a bargain with yourself to set time aside later in the day to return and mentally retrieve the piece of paper and readdress the problem you wrote upon it. If you find this sort of visualisation difficult, then use a real piece of paper and an envelope, going through the same process of writing down the problem, putting it away physically and mentally, and then returning later to retrieve it.

Obviously, you can't employ this sort of strategy while actually climbing. You have to develop the ability to ignore distractions – to treat them as irrelevant. You can practise this while bouldering or climbing, by trying to concentrate on what you are doing while your 'friends' try and distract you with their witty observations on your climbing technique, personal failings etc. Concentrate on each move in turn, trying as always to climb as precisely and beautifully as possible.

Visualisation is the art of using your imagination to rehearse actual activities. Children have no difficulty in conjuring up whole imaginary worlds, often in amazing detail, but this ability is often lost as we 'mature' into adulthood. Recapturing this skill can be worked at, and when fully developed is a very powerful tool. To succeed with this technique requires the ability to relax and concentrate at the same time.

Start simply by sitting in a familiar room, closing your eyes and relaxing for a couple of minutes. Then conjure up the image of an object, such as a vase, that was in your line of sight when you sat down. Make the image as detailed as possible, in full Technicolor. Then try to imagine what it looks like from the far side. Open your eyes and see how accurate you were, and, if not quite right, try again. Once you can visualise objects with accuracy, add other facets such as the feel of touching it, or the sound of flicking the rim.

If you can manage this with objects without difficulty, expand your repertoire by imagining yourself getting up from your chair and walking into another room. Imagine how everything will look, sound and smell. Graduate to imagining yourself doing simple tasks, such as making a sandwich or a cup of coffee. This ability does not come easily to most people and needs regular practice. Your images must be as detailed as possible. Once you can accurately imagine yourself doing day-to-day tasks, introduce the way you feel while doing them. When you can achieve this, it's time to go climbing.

You are going to visualise doing a familiar route. Sit down and relax for a couple of minutes. Then visualise how it feels to warm up, put on your boots, tie on your chalk bag and step up to the rock face. Try not to imagine it as if it happened in the past, but that it is happening now, in the present. What's the weather like? A pleasant summer evening with just a hint of a breeze bringing the drone of distant traffic and the metallic clink and clatter of climbers on other routes. You step up to the rock and touch the coarse gritstone. It's still warm from the day's sun. Chalk up and reach for the opening holds. Stepping up on the small positive edge on the left brings a two-finger pocket for the left hand just within reach – you feel perfectly in balance, perfectly in control. Imagine each move in turn, climbing smoothly and effortlessly up to the crux and powering through this to the top. Imagine how it feels, the pump in your forearms, the sweat on your brow, the elation of success ... For you, it may be a limestone or granite route, the important thing is the detail with which you bring it to life.

Once you have developed the ability to visualise previous experiences with all your senses, you can start trying to accurately imagine things you haven't yet done, and then manipulate them to your advantage. If trying a new route, assimilate information from whatever sources are available and then feed it into your visualisation, to make it as accurate as possible. Try to imagine yourself approaching the crux feeling powerful and confident and then cruising it with style. If you work routes before red pointing them, you will already know the moves, so stringing them together in your mind, visualising a successful outcome, should not be too difficult.

For on sight leading, practise at the wall or while bouldering by looking at the moves and working out how you are going to complete the sequence in your mind. Watch Stefan Glowacz or Robyn Erbesfield at a competition, the way they look at the holds and rehearse the moves in their minds, working out which will be a layaway, which an undercut, where to cut loose etc., before setting off. Sometimes they get it wrong, but among those who do well, the ability to visualise seems well advanced.

Visualisation can be used to rebuild your confidence after failure. Go over your performance again, including everything that went wrong. Then repeat the visualisation, but this time build in a successful outcome, with all the feelings that this would produce. This will help to reduce the level of anxiety at your next attempt.

Another way of helping performance is to make affirmative statements to yourself before and during the climb. Probably the best known is Mohammed Ali's 'I am the greatest'. These statements can be used to bolster yourself as the going gets tough while training (mutter 'Lean, mean climbing machine' to yourself while running up that last hill or doing that last set of pull ups). They can also be used as part of the mental rehearsal when preparing for a hard route or competition: 'When I am in the holding area I *will* feel calm and fully prepared.' 'When I am at the foot of the route I *will* feel confident and powerful.' 'When I approach the crux I *will* feel a surge of new energy.' 'I *will* hit that finger pocket exactly right at the crux dyno.' These are just examples of the sort of statements that you can use. You will have to find the words and images that work specifically for you. They should be repeated frequently during the day in the run up to an important event and should be worked into your visualisations. Try to make them as positive as possible, i.e. not 'I must not make any mistakes' but 'I *will* not make any mistakes and *will* climb beautifully.'

You can make up a tape of music that inspires you and insert these positive statements in-between tracks. A few encouraging words from your regular climbing friends and/or partner ('I know you can do it' etc.) also don't go amiss. You can put in reminders for yourself of anything you think is important and you may forget ('Don't forget my lucky tights'. 'Check the flow of competitors to be able to judge when to warm up'). You can play this tape to yourself while travelling around in the car, or lying in the bath, several times a day during the week before the important event. Don't forget to take the tape and your Walkman with you, and play it while warming up.

To help you tune in to this sort of situation some people find it also helps to develop a pre-climb/performance ritual. This may involve getting changed into your favourite climbing attire, using the same warm-up routine, listening to the same music, all in a familiar, specific sequence. For this to have an effect, you should follow your routine whenever you go climbing or to a leading wall.

To get the most of any mental rehearsal technique you need to practise **regularly**. Five minutes a day is better than half an hour one day and nothing more for a week. Above all it should be enjoyable. If you are getting bored and irritated, it is time to look for a different technique that you can live with.

8   Nutrition

There is probably more nonsense talked about the role of nutrition in training than almost any other aspect of preparation in sport. This is perhaps surprising when energy consumption and the body's requirements for carbohydrate, fat and protein and the various vitamins and minerals that make up a diet can be fairly accurately calculated for any one individual.

To reduce the science of nutrition to its most basic, in order to survive you need oxygen, water, some carbohydrate, a mixture of ten essential amino acids (from protein), a small amount of fat, including three essential fatty acids, thirteen vitamins and eighteen elements, such as calcium, magnesium, sodium, potassium, etc.

Carbohydrates are the sugars and starches found in foods such as fruit, bread, rice, pasta and potatoes (as well as the white poison some people put in their tea and coffee) that are broken down to simple molecules and absorbed during digestion and stored as glycogen in the muscles and the liver. Glycogen in muscles is the principal store of energy during aerobic activity and, in someone who is relatively well trained, will sustain activity at near maximal rates for only about an hour. Liver glycogen stores act as a reserve and are used first during fasting (including not eating while asleep). Liver glycogen stores are rapidly restored by eating carbohydrate but replenishment of muscle glycogen after a maximum, prolonged effort takes about twenty-four hours.

Carbohydrate provides 4.1 kcal of energy for each gramme and should be the principal source of energy in a training or competing athlete.

Proteins are made up of chains of complex molecules called amino acids, and make up muscle as well as numerous other structures in the body. For most people in our society their principal source of protein is from meat. Some amino acids can be synthesised by the body and some cannot and so become 'essential'. Luckily for vegetarians, these essential amino acids are also found in dairy products and in nuts, pulses, beans etc., though not in such abundant quantities.

Although protein produces 5.3 kcal/g, it is not an important source of energy in the body, and therefore much less is required in a day. About 1.5g per kilo of your weight (if you are relatively lean) per day is sufficient. This contributes about 15 per cent of total energy intake.

Fats are highly calorific, producing 9.3 kcal/g. They are required to produce a number of vital structures in the body, such as cell membranes and hormones. There is some evidence that a diet high in saturated fat and cholesterol can contribute to heart disease, and so it is generally recommended to restrict this component of your diet to less than 30 per cent of your total energy requirement.

Using the information above will help you interpret the nutritional information on the side of the packaging of various food stuffs when working out the energy content of your diet. This information needs to be looked at critically as it can often be misleading. The calories contained in unpackaged or unlabelled foods can be looked up in any dietary 'calorie counter'.

Vitamins (vital amines) are compounds that the body requires in order to carry out certain metabolic processes. There is nothing magical about them and when taken in overdose some of them can be positively harmful. There is no really sound evidence that vitamin requirements are raised in training athletes and, providing you eat a reasonably varied diet, it is unlikely you will become vitamin deficient. There is some theoretical advantage, however, in making sure your intake of antioxidants (Vitamins A, C and E) is above minimum requirements by taking supplements.

Manipulating dietary input is now a reasonably precise art and plays a part in maximising performance in endurance events, by altering the body's various energy systems. There are a lot of claims made about this wonder diet and that magic herbal extract, but very few of them stand up to close scrutiny. You can save yourself a lot of money and stay healthy by following simple and common-sense guidelines.

In general we eat too much fat, and too much salt. Avoid fatty cuts of meat and don't fry food. Don't add salt to your food. There is an adequate amount of naturally occurring salt in a lot of food stuffs, even if you are a salt junkie and can't taste it! It is important, particularly when doing a lot of training or climbing, to keep well hydrated, so drink plenty. Avoid 'empty calories', foods such as white sugar and bread which, although containing a lot of calories in the form of carbohydrate, contain little else of nutritional value and very little, if any roughage. Eat plenty of fresh fruit and vegetables. Moderate your alcohol consumption.

What everyone wants to know is both how much they should eat and what their diet should consist of. It is impossible to give an accurate answer that will be suitable for everyone. Obviously, each individual is unique and, with different metabolic rates and energy expenditures, individual requirements may vary enormously.

No single food can supply all the essential components needed to keep fit and well, which is why having a variety of foods in your diet is so important. Foodstuffs can be roughly divided into five different groups:

1 Cereals – wheat, maize, rice, etc.
2 Vegetables and fruit
3 Meat/fish/eggs
4 Dairy products
5 Butter/oil/margarine

Generally one needs a mixture of the various groups. The so-called 'nutrition pyramid' is a widely used model which

Figure 1

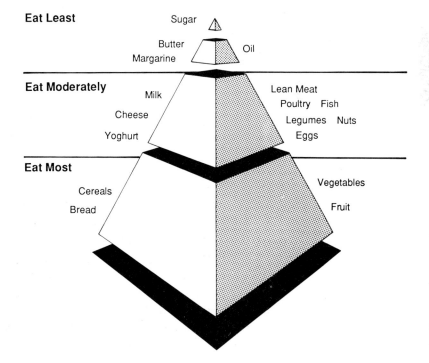

65

gives you a rough guide to how you should divide up your food intake (Fig 1). Vegetarians will obviously miss out on group 3 but can replace animal protein with dairy products or, if a vegan, with a wide variety of pulses, beans, nuts etc. Indeed, a lacto-ovo-vegetarian diet (a vegetarian who eats eggs and dairy products) has much to recommend it as a method of obtaining ideal training nutrition.

The average male requires total energy of about 2,500 kcal (10.6 MJ) a day and the average female about $\frac{4}{5}$ of this. Training may increase energy requirement by 30 per cent or more. Once in training, an athlete (or even a reasonably fit climber!) develops a higher resting metabolic rate, which also increases basic energy requirements.

For a climber in moderate training, the total daily energy intake should be broken down so that about 55 per cent comes from carbohydrates, 30 per cent from fat and 15 per cent from protein. If training more than about ninety minutes a day, it is recommended that the percentage of calories from carbohydrate is increased to 60–65 per cent. This can work out as a large quantity of food, and may require a change from the normal three meals a day, to four or five, so as to reduce each meal to an eatable amount.

Figure 2

For climbing, particularly at the elite end of the sport

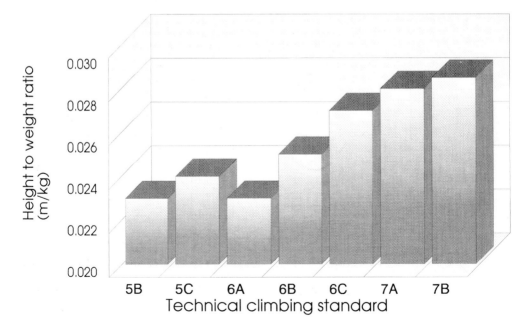

66

where small increases in power-to-weight ratio can be critical to success or failure, it is important to keep your weight down. The less you weigh the less effort you will have to expend, and the less strength and power you need to move up the rock against the forces of gravity. It can be seen in Fig 2 that power-to-weight ratio and skin-fold thickness (this is the measurement of subcutaneous fat and therefore a reflection of how much surplus you are carrying) correlate very strongly with climbing performance.

If you are overweight and wish to lose it there are many different types of diet that can all be relatively successful, given the discipline to see them through. If training hard and trying to lose weight at the same time, reduce daily calorie intake by about 500 kcal from your estimated requirements and find a diet that maintains a high percentage of carbohydrate to provide energy. This helps to preserve fuel reserves for training and staves off hunger. Diets that have a low carbohydrate intake are associated with a loss of muscle mass and cause a reduction in your capacity for power and endurance.

Crash dieting before competitions or a long-coveted and hard red point is to be avoided, as this can produce a metabolic state which impairs strength and endurance. It is obvious, however, that when reducing training in the few days before a hard climb or competition, a corresponding and appropriate reduction in energy intake is necessary in order to avoid sudden weight gain. It is important, however, to maintain the percentage of carbohydrate intake during this period.

To maintain a low weight, especially as one gets older, is not easy and takes a permanent alteration in eating habits and constant vigilance. This may be harder for some than others, as the propensity for obesity may be decided in infancy, with fat babies developing a greater potential for becoming fat adults. Care is needed, especially in adolescence, as it is easy to get into the downward spiral leading to anorexia nervosa or bulimia nervosa, the two 'slimming diseases'.

EATING BEFORE TRAINING, CLIMBING OR COMPETING

Carbohydrate, protein and fat are all digested and absorbed by the body at different rates. It takes about two hours for the energy from carbohydrate to become available, five hours for protein, and eight hours for fat. Protein and fat slow down the absorption of carbohydrate if they are mixed together in a meal.

This knowledge can be used when planning your training sessions. If you are training twice a day (!), the plan would be to eat a breakfast high in carbohydrate and low in protein and fat (a fairly typical modern Western breakfast of cereal with skimmed milk, fruit and fruit juice, wholemeal toast and jam [easy on the polyunsaturated margarine] is ideal) and then start training two hours later for about two to three hours. Lunch should be of a similar make up and then a two-hour rest and another two-hour training session. This could be followed by tea and then an evening meal to make up your total daily requirement.

This regime can also be used for doing red points, substituting two hours' climbing for each training session. If this is impractical, or you don't like eating a meal during the day, or are even doing a traditional, multi-pitch route (!), eat a bigger breakfast with a higher fat and protein content so the energy is released more slowly, and then snack during the day as you feel like it. Avoid large doses of refined carbohydrate, such as chocolate bars, in the hour before training/climbing/competing as this affects the functioning of the hormone insulin (which normally controls the level of blood sugar) leading to a more rapid depletion of muscle glycogen.

Don't forget that it is important to keep well hydrated both when training and climbing. It is advisable to drink a couple of glasses of water or fruit juice in the hour before training or climbing. After heavy training or climbing sessions, particularly in the summer, you may develop a considerable fluid deficit. The stomach can only absorb about one litre an hour, so aim to fully rehydrate over several hours.

If competing, the same principles apply. A pre-competition meal should replenish your glycogen stores, make sure you are fully hydrated and help prevent hunger and nausea. If you are likely to compete early on, eat breakfast as above about two to three hours before your turn on the wall. Otherwise eat a bigger breakfast with more protein and fat, and then top up if necessary with a high-carbohydrate snack, such as a banana washed down with a glass of skimmed milk or fruit juice, taken at least one-and-a-half hours before competing. If pre-competition nerves rob you of your appetite, you may find it easier to tolerate one of the liquid foods like Complan, sipped slowly during your hours in the isolation zone.

Recovery from the effects of hard competition/climbing/training is a matter of replacing the glycogen fuel stores in your muscles that have been burnt up during effort. To produce the most rapid restocking of glycogen, you need to start replacing it immediately exercise has stopped, by eating carbohydrate-rich snacks or drinking carbohydrate-rich fluids. Even waiting a couple of hours before starting this process can delay recovery and prejudice your performance on the following day. When recovering from a very big effort you need to increase your carbohydrate intake to about 10g per kilogramme of your body weight over the immediate following twenty-four hours.

Finally, don't forget you are what you eat, so if you eat junk food...

9   Putting It All Together

Hopefully you have now read and digested some of the information in preceding chapters and are now ready to try and put together the various elements of a training programme. There is no panacea, no routine, that is guaranteed to turn any ageing, v.diff leader into a competition superstar. Your personalised training programme will depend on many things, such as the time you are prepared to devote to it, your own strengths, weaknesses and physical make-up and, perhaps most importantly, your will to succeed.

In this short chapter I will outline some basic training regimes catering for various levels of skill and ambition and then you will have to fine tune them to your own requirements. Common to all these is a basic background of a level of aerobic fitness based on three half-hour sessions of jogging/cycling/swimming/aerobics a week, and sticking to the nutritional advice previously given. **Any training programme will require three to four months of dedication to see much in the way of improvement.**

For the novice or average climber, the first stage is to develop endurance and basic strength, concentrating predominantly on gym (and some fingerboard) work, from where you can launch yourself onwards (and upwards!) with a level of protection against catastrophic injury. This stage should take about eight weeks and the exercises can be found in the chapters on gym work and climbing. To see real improvement this presumes a minimum of three training sessions (of about one to two hours) a week and a morning/afternoon at the climbing wall/crag. Each session will be preceded by a run-through the stretching routine as part of the warm-up. From this solid base you can begin to concentrate on developing power and honing your climbing skills, gradually introducing more climbing as the weeks go by, but maintaining at least once-weekly power and endurance sessions. Always make sure you are feeling fresh before pushing yourself in a strength or power session because, if your muscles are tired, you will not perform well and you increase your chance of injury.

This pattern of training can be seen in graph form in Fig 1. Three months is really a minimum to aim to peak for a particular route or event, and a longer time period is better – the graph can be stretched out appropriately. It is difficult to maintain a peak level of performance for long periods and most athletes will organise their training schedules to contain periods of 'relative rest' and light training that occur after a period of peaking. This usually works out at about 10 per cent of total training time and during this time your performance will take a turn for the worse. Stay cool, and accept that it is necessary for your body to recover before the next phase of training. This is a good time to concentrate on your stretching and mental skills.

If you are a full-time climber then training can be a little more intensive. The biggest danger for the keen and committed is usually overtraining, leading to overuse injury. Certainly in the UK, I see the results of a lot of bad training technique and I can't emphasise enough that it is important to train properly. For the dedicated climber the same general

Figure 1
The Training Plan

Training Intensity

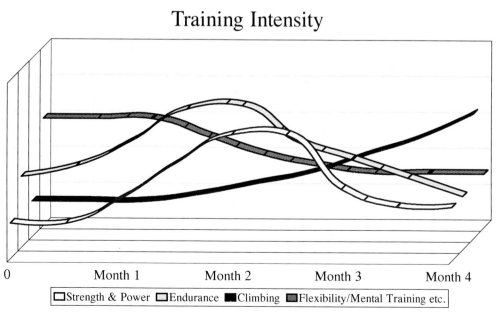

| 0 | Month 1 | Month 2 | Month 3 | Month 4 |

☐ Strength & Power ☐ Endurance ■ Climbing ■ Flexibility/Mental Training etc.

(N.B. remember to wind right down in the week before the big event)

pattern as described above can be adopted, but obviously more can be packed into the same time period.

Below is an example of the sort of training regime that could be employed, aiming to peak over a three-month cycle, training twice a day, five days a week. This will not suit everyone and will need fine tuning for each individual. 'Light bouldering' means at the crag or wall, with relatively easy problems or routes on reasonably large holds, to help prevent muscle stiffness after previous hard muscle work.

	a.m.	p.m.
Monday	stretching + run/swim/aerobics etc.	rest + mental training
Tuesday	strength/power workout	light bouldering
Wednesday	endurance workout	light bouldering
Thursday	stretching + run/swim/aerobics etc.	rest + mental training
Friday	strength/power workout	light bouldering
Saturday	endurance workout	rest
Sunday	rest	climb

As you start to get closer to the goal you are aiming for, one of the endurance and one of the power sessions can be dropped and on-sighting/red pointing substituted. In the final run up to a big route or competition, the week prior to the event should be very light, with a forty-eight-hour rest before the big moment. Use this time to mentally focus and 'tune in' on the battle to come. Don't forget to reduce calorie intake appropriately during the period to prevent sudden weight gain.

I must repeat that this is only an example of a training plan and will not suit everyone. Using the material in this book I hope you will be able to construct a plan that will suit your needs whatever the time you have available or your ultimate goals.

10   Injuries

Injury is something we all dread and would like to avoid if possible. It comes in many forms. If you fall a long way through the air and hit something solid while bouldering, soloing or climbing at the wall, you're going to get hurt. The different types of injury one can sustain in this situation would fill a fair-sized medical text book! The important thing is that we all should have at least a working knowledge of basic, life-saving first aid – your life or your partner's life may one day depend on it.

Having said that, I'll get down to the main purpose of this chapter, which is to give some brief advice on the recognition and treatment of training and overuse injuries, and some hints on how to avoid them in the first place! It must be stressed, however, that no matter how brilliant this chapter is, it is no substitute for good 'hands on' professional diagnosis and treatment.

Figure 1
Sites of Soft
Tissue Injury
in the Arm

Most injuries that occur when training or climbing involve the 'soft tissues' – the muscles, their tendons that attach them to the bone, and the ligaments that keep the joints stable. Muscles and tendons can be injured anywhere along their length from origin to insertion (Fig 1).

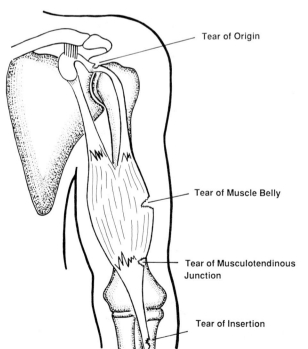

Tear of Origin

Tear of Muscle Belly

Tear of Musculotendinous Junction

Tear of Insertion

The symptom that tell you that something has gone wrong is PAIN, and means that you have subjected some part of your body to a stress it is inadequately prepared for, or incapable of coping with. This often occurs suddenly, as in trying to stop a fall or trying to lift too heavy a weight, but can occur more insidiously when performing repetitive, unbalanced training routines, without giving the body time to recover between sessions.

WHAT HAPPENS DURING INJURY?

At the moment of injury, tearing of some structure or structures occurs. This inevitably ruptures small blood vessels, causing bleeding. The damaged tissue attracts more fluid and the end result is swelling and bruising. You can see this happening if the injury is close to the skin. This swelling can actually slow down healing by physically holding apart the ends of the tear, making a larger defect.

After about forty-eight hours the blood and damaged tissue is gradually replaced by new cells which make the fibrous tissue that forms a scar. In the case of a small muscle tear, reasonable healing will have taken place by about ten days, but a scar really takes a minimum of three months to reach its full strength. This time interval is of course relatively unimportant when only a very small percentage of the muscle, ligament or tendon is involved, but becomes progressively more important the greater the extent of the injury.

Acute injury (injury that occurs suddenly), commonly referred to as a sprain, is usually divided into three grades. The first and most common type is when there is a tear of about 10 per cent of the muscle, tendon or ligament. Although this type of injury is painful, it will recover with the minimum of interference in about ten days.

The second type is more serious and involves a significant, but less than total, tear and will need medical attention. These usually take between eight and twelve weeks to heal. The third and most serious type of soft-tissue injury, where there is complete rupture of muscle, tendon or ligament, cannot heal properly without medical intervention, usually in the form of surgery or prolonged protective bracing.

Chronic injury, i.e. injury that persists for a long time, is almost always self-inflicted and is due to returning to climbing or training before an injury is fully healed or rehabilitated. Because the muscle or tendon is still weak, it is re-injured much more easily and gradually a vicious cycle develops.

Overuse injury occurs in a slightly different way. Repeated overload, as in an unbalanced training programme with inadequate rests, produces microtears within the overused structure – just as a piece of steel or concrete will eventually fatigue and break if it is repeatedly subjected to large loads. At first, symptoms are minor and usually occur as an aching for a couple of hours after exercise. Because early symptoms resolve fairly quickly, the same vicious circle is easily entered into. Tendons, being relatively inelastic, are particularly susceptible to this 'fatigue failure'.

In humans this type of injury causes inflammation, producing such problems as tendinitis (inflammation of the tendons) and tenosynovitis (inflammation of the lining of the tendons), which, if not treated early and properly, can become chronic. It is then very difficult, if not impossible, to cure, requiring months of rehabilitation.

MUSCLE SORENESS

A common affliction is 'delayed muscle soreness', the stiffness and soreness of whole muscles or groups of muscles, which comes on usually between twenty-four and forty-eight hours after hard climbing or training, and may last several days. There are several theories as to the cause of this, but it seems to be due to tears at a microscopic level within the individual muscle cells. It usually comes on after the start of a training programme, or when suddenly accelerating one.

Preventing muscle soreness is easy! Just follow a graduated training programme, on a regular basis, with a proper warm-up every time. Beginners should start with a programme of light loads and low repetitions and increase reps only by about 10 per cent at a time. Large increases in loads should be avoided. If you have been imprudent, a few days' rest clears it up. Light exercise may speed things up, but some people find this too painful.

TREATMENT OF INJURIES

I cannot stress enough that proper treatment follows accurate diagnosis. All acute, minor, soft-tissue injuries, however, can initially be treated with the same sort of first aid. Major soft-tissue injuries can also be treated along these lines for the first few hours, while seeking professional help. The magic word is RICE. This stands for Rest, Ice, Compression and Elevation and should be started as soon as possible after injury.

Rest is important and is all too often ignored! Further use of an injured structure within the first forty-eight hours only causes more bleeding and swelling, and therefore delays healing. Rest for longer periods is required with more serious injuries. Rest does not mean you have to retire to your sick bed. Only the injured part has to be protected, and you may continue to train any other bit of you that is still in one piece.

Ice, or anything very cold, applied as soon as possible after injury and then intermittently for the first twenty-four to thirty-six hours, helps reduce the amount of bleeding and swelling, and therefore speeds up the healing process. It also helps reduce the amount of pain. Ice cubes in a plastic bag or a pack of frozen vegetables (which can be re-frozen in between treatments and used for future injuries – once used this way, it is not recommended to eat them!) are perfectly adequate. It must be applied for long enough periods to be effective. During the first few hours it should be applied in fifteen-minute periods (or until the skin is numb, whichever comes first) for about thirty minutes out of each hour. Tolerance to this form of therapy varies widely between individuals, but once the skin begins to blush it has been applied long enough. It is important to protect the skin with baby oil or a thin layer of damp cloth, as ice can cause burns (this is especially important when using stuff straight from the freezer, as this will be below freezing point). **Cold therapy should not be used if you have any problems with your circulation.**

Compression in the form of strapping or elasticated bandages also helps decrease the bleeding and swelling by raising the pressure within the damaged area. This must be done properly, applying an even pressure, from well below to well above the site of injury. Too much pressure can cut off the circulation beyond the strapping and tends to cause that bit to drop off with gangrene, so be careful! If you don't know what you're doing, get somebody who does to do it for you. Strapping can also help healing by drawing the torn ends of the damaged tissue closer together.

Elevation helps excess fluid drain back into the body by the effect of gravity. For a foot or ankle injury, this means resting with your foot higher than your knee and hip, and for a hand or wrist injury, a high sling with your hand on the opposite shoulder.

On no account should heat treatment or massage be used in the forty-eight hours following injury, as they only cause further bleeding, making the injury worse.

IF IN DOUBT SEEK A MEDICAL OPINION ABOUT ANY INJURY NOT SHOWING SIGNIFICANT IMPROVEMENT AFTER FORTY-EIGHT HOURS.

After the first forty-eight hours, injured tissues still need support, but now you can introduce local heat treatment to help disperse any accumulated swelling. 'Contrast bathing' is an effective way of doing this – first apply ice, as above, for three to four minutes, then immediately apply a hot pack (a hot water bottle at a suitable temperature can be used) for one to two minutes and repeat this process five times. The whole process should be performed several times during the day for two or three days. Physiotherapists, when using short-wave diathermy and some forms of ultrasound, are basically applying heat, but in a more penetrating and effective way. Heat creams are of no proven benefit.

Heat treatment also helps relieve pain and enables you to start gently exercising the affected part. You should initially aim to regain a larger range of pain-free movements of the injured area, before beginning any form of exercise against resistance.

There is some evidence that non-steroidal anti-inflammatory drugs, such as ibuprofen, which you can buy at a chemist, can help speed up the healing of acute minor soft-tissue injuries, although there is some debate about this. They do have side effects, however, and are to be avoided if you suffer from indigestion or stomach ulcers – read the warnings on the packet.

For *muscle* injuries, rehabilitative exercise should begin

as soon as a large, pain-free range of movements have been regained. Work out which movement has caused the injury, or was the painful one, and aim to specifically strengthen the muscle that has been damaged. *Always* start by gently warming up and performing stretching exercises within the limits of pain. Weights should be used carefully, starting with static, isometric, low-load exercises, progressing to dynamic exercises and then gradually increasing the resistance. This may well take several weeks. A return to climbing should really be delayed until full, pain-free power has been regained. During rehabilitation from injury, *pain* should always be your guide – exercise should be increased until you find the level at which it starts to cause pain, and then carried out at just below the pain threshold.

You are not doing yourself any good pushing through pain when recovering from injury. In fact you will be doing yourself harm!

Tendon injuries are more serious than minor muscle tears and often take much longer to heal. If there is any indication that a tendon is not working properly and is very painful, medical attention should be sought *immediately*. If a tendon has ruptured, it needs to be repaired or treated within thirty-six to forty-eight hours to get the best result. Even partial tears need to be treated with respect.

For minor injuries, after the initial first aid treatment, rehabilitation is best carried out by progressive gentle stretching exercises and a weight-training programme, progressing through isometric, isotonic and finally a phase consisting predominantly of *eccentric* exercise (for an explanation of eccentric exercise see Chapter 2), tailored to the particular tendon involved. The eccentric exercises should start with a low weight and at the slow speed. The speed is gradually increased until the particular exercise can be performed at maximum speed without provoking pain. The weight is then increased and the process started again. All exercise programmes following injury should always be preceded by a proper warm up and are best supervised by a chartered physiotherapist with an interest in sports injuries.

'Transverse frictions' are often mentioned in conjunction with tendon injuries, although they are also useful in ligament sprains. The technique basically consists of rubbing very hard on the most tender spot, across the line of the tendon or ligament. It is used mainly in chronic injuries of the elbow, shoulder and knee. It is often exquisitely painful, and is best performed by someone you're not too attached to!

Minor damage to *ligaments* cause pain on stressing a joint, more serious injury leaves a feeling of instability, i.e. the affected joints feels 'wobbly'. Surprisingly, complete rupture may be almost painless, although instability is quite marked. Minor ligament sprains, which do not compromise the stability of the joint, only need to be supported or splinted for two to three weeks. Providing the involved ligament is not stressed, treatment need not stop movement (see finger injuries below). On return to activity, the affected joint is helped by appropriate protective strapping (diagrams can be found in most sports injury text books). More serious tears initially need six to eight weeks of protection, and complete ruptures often need surgical repair.

Overuse injuries usually affect the origin of the muscle, the junction of muscle and tendon, the tendon itself or the point of insertion of the tendon into bone. They can be very difficult to treat and are best avoided! Warning signs start with the occurrence of pain for a couple of hours after activity, at the same site each time. This progresses to pain which starts during exercise and lasts for a couple of hours afterwards. If allowed to, this will gradually deteriorate over days and weeks, until pain is continuous. By this stage treatment is difficult and a cure very uncertain.

Rest is the initial and vital ingredient. I know this is difficult to do when you're suffering 'adrenaline withdrawal', but you'll save yourself a lot of grief if you treat it properly at the start! In the early stages properly warming up, stretching, reducing activity by 50 per cent and taking a short course of non-steroidal anti-inflammatory tablets (see above) may be sufficient, but in the later stages complete avoidance of any pain-inducing activity for up to a year may be necessary. Ice massage of the affected area after exercise is also very helpful in the very early stages. An eccentric exercise programme, as outlined previously, is a current favourite among rehabilitative treatments, and may be coupled with steroid injections (not the ones that give you big muscles!) by a suitably qualified doctor. As a last resort surgery may be the only alternative, even though the results are often unpredictable.

WHERE TO GET HELP

Treating yourself for anything other than minor injuries, especially if you're not sure what exactly is wrong, is a bit risky and I wouldn't recommend it. Proper treatment can only be carried out once an accurate diagnosis has been made and for that you often need a professional.

The RICE first aid regime can be carried out whatever the soft-tissue injury, but then where do you go for help? If you suspect anything serious, the only place to go is the local hospital casualty department. This must be within the first forty-eight hours. Don't forget, you're young and fit and among the 'walking wounded', so try and be patient and tactful, even if there is a long wait.

Many cities now have specialist sports clinics where expertise is on hand but many of these are private and you will have to pay. Ask around to see if there is a local consultant with an interest in sports injuries to whom you can be referred. Otherwise, unless your local GP has a particular interest in sports injuries, a chartered physiotherapist is probably the best person to consult. They are specialists in the treatment of soft-tissue injury. Some hospital physiotherapy departments have a direct-referral system so you can be sent directly from your doctor, or you may have to be referred from a casualty department. If the worst comes to the worst, you can always shell out the cash and go privately.

Physiotherapists have a large array of equipment to make you better and are pretty good at putting their finger on the problem. If the damage is too serious for them to mend, they will usually refer you to the appropriate doctor.

SPECIFIC INJURIES

The Lower Limb

Injuries of the lower limb in climbing seem to be uncommon. However, I'll mention the ones I've come across.

Abductor Strain. These are the muscles on the insides of your thighs, particularly vulnerable in wide bridging, when a sudden, acute pain up near your groin means you've stretched a bridge too far. Treatment is along the above lines; if not allowed to heal, it can be very difficult to cure, requiring a combination of physiotherapy, steroid injections and even surgery, with no guarantee of success.

Hamstring Strain. These are the muscles at the back of the thigh that are particularly vulnerable during heel hooking. Unlike the adductors, which are usually affected at their origin in the groin, they commonly tear at the musculo-tendinous junction down near the back of the knee. Treatment is along standard lines for muscle injury.

Patella Tendinitis. Causes pain just below the knee cap, usually caused initially by a strenuous rockover. This also can become chronic, so be careful. Treatment plan is as for tendon injuries.

Meniscal Injuries. These are most common in footballers and are usually known as a 'torn cartilage' in the knee. They are most vulnerable when moving up on to a high rockover, when the knee is hyperflexed. A small twist can then tear the posterior part of the cartilage. This causes pain on the joint line, swelling, which usually comes on after several hours, and often an inability to straighten or fully bend the knee. This requires surgical treatment. Torn cartilages can now be removed, or even repairs made, through a telescope-like instrument inserted into the knee through a tiny incision. This type of surgery is not universally available, so make sure you are referred to an appropriate specialist.

The Upper Limb

The upper limb takes most of the punishment in modern climbing. In a survey I carried out, 85 per cent of the injuries were in this area. You can divide it roughly into three regions: the shoulder, the elbow, and the hand and wrist.

THE SHOULDER

Some form of rotator cuff injury seems to be the commonest

problem. The rotator cuff is the group of muscles that surround the shoulder joint, giving it stability and moving the upper arm. Acute, minor tears of this often occur and should receive the standard treatment of such injuries. Complete tears are rare, but inability to move the arm normally, associated with a lot of pain, needs a hospital opinion.

Supraspinatus Tendonitis. This is inflammation of the tendon of supraspinatus, the muscle that initiates movement of the arm sideways away, from your body. It is usually caused by prolonged and repeated use, or overload of the shoulder muscles, with the arm above shoulder height. It can also exist in a chronic form caused by incomplete healing after minor tears. It causes pain and tenderness over the front part of the shoulder joint, pain on rotating the shoulder out, and pain in an arc between 60 and 120 degrees when lifting the arm up and away from your side. Rest is the most vital part of treatment. Once pain has settled, a stretching and eccentric exercise programme should be followed. Physiotherapy with ultrasound and transverse frictions is very useful. Non-steroidal anti-inflammatory drugs may help but it may require steroid injections. If all else fails, surgery may be of benefit.

Impingement Syndrome. This is now recognised to be a common cause of problems in sports involving the use of the arm above shoulder height. The tendons that pass over the top of the shoulder joint pass through a tunnel between shoulder blade and collar bone above and the ball and socket of the joint below. Overuse, in the form of repetitive overhead stress, causes a mechanical irritation against the front edge of this tunnel, causing inflammation. This inflammation makes the tissue swell, further restricting the available space and thereby causing more impingement and a vicious circle is set up.

It is now recognised that, in a lot of cases, muscle imbalance around the shoulder either initiates or contributes to this problem. If there is a relative weakness in the muscles that stabilise the scapula (shoulder blade) it leads to the head of the humerus slipping forward in its socket during movements, jamming the rotator cuff up against the ligament that forms the front edge of the tunnel.

There is usually an insidious onset of soreness in the front of the shoulder. This is at first merely annoying, but as time passes and the overhead stress continues, it gradually becomes more severe and becomes a constant toothache-like pain. Pain is felt when the arm is swung forward and up as far as it will go. Treatment, as usual, starts with rest. Ice massage after exercise in the early stages is useful. Physiotherapy with ultrasound is very good at reducing the inflammation and steroid injections may be necessary. Rehabilitation is outlined below. Surgery, aiming to increase the space through which the tendons pass, has achieved some success when all else has failed.

Rehabilitation for both these conditions consists initially of isometric exercises, and then progresses to an active exercise programme aimed at correcting any imbalance between the pairs of muscles which move the shoulder in different directions, i.e. forwards and backwards or rotating in and out (Figs 2–5) *always preceded by a proper warm up*, keeping the shoulder blade as still as possible. Correction of training practice to increase the strength of the stabilisers of the scapula is often a vital part of rehabilitation.

THE ELBOW

The elbow joint acts as the anchor for the muscles that move the hand and wrist. When these muscles are overused or have too much strain put on them, it is very often the elbow that feels the pain.

'Tennis Elbow', Lateral Epicondylitis. With the palm facing forward, pain from tennis elbow is felt on the outside of the joint. It arises from the origin of the muscles which steady the wrist in the slightly bent-back position that is necessary to gain maximum power from the finger flexors. Treatment is by ice massage followed by stretching exercises (Chapter 4) performed frequently during the day. 'Transverse frictions' (this is very painful!) and ultrasound may help if you can get them. Progressive muscle strengthening of the dorsiflexors of the wrist and brachioradialis (Figs 6–9) will help prevent recurrence. You can buy tennis-elbow braces in the shops but they don't always help and, anyway, you shouldn't resume climbing or training before it has healed. Steroid injections may be necessary in resistant cases and surgery is a last resort.

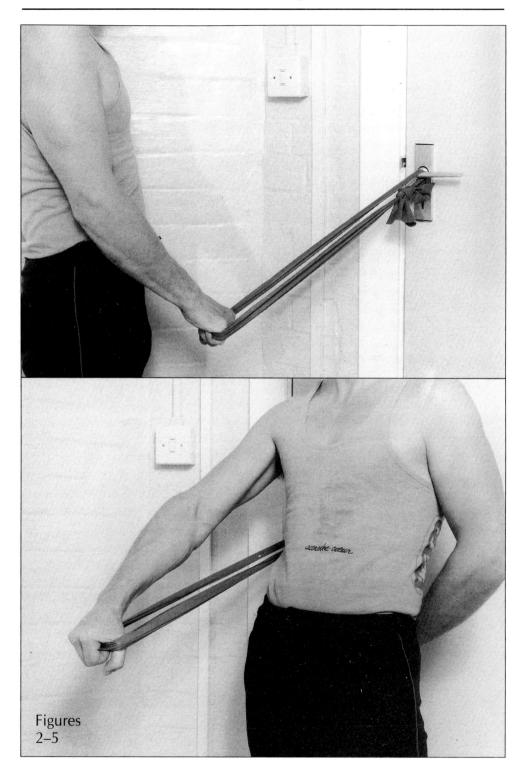

Figures
2–5

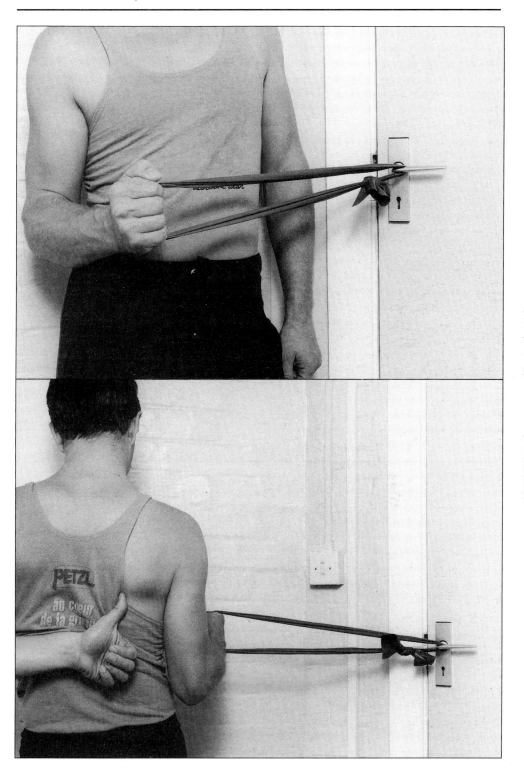

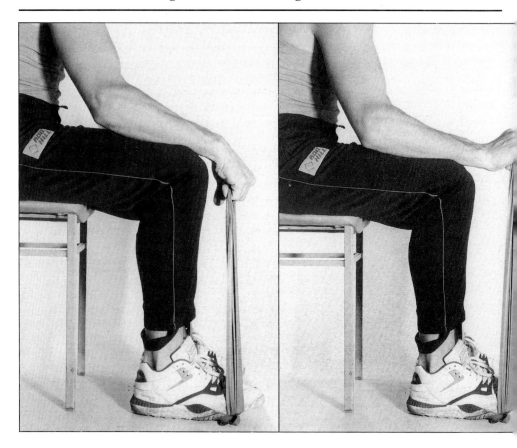

Figures
6–9

'Golfer's Elbow', Medial Epicondylitis. This is basically the same as the above but it affects the inside of the elbow where the wrist flexors arise. Treatment is the same except the opposite muscles are stretched and strengthened.

'Climber's Elbow', Anterior Elbow Pain. This affects climbers who do a lot of repetitive traversing and causes pain in the middle of the front of the elbow joint. It seems to arise from the insertion of the brachialis muscle and is a form of tendinitis. Treatment is along standard lines – rest, ice, massage, an eccentric exercise programme and ultrasound.

THE HAND AND WRIST

The bits at the end of your arms come in for the greatest punishment. They have to be capable of transmitting great

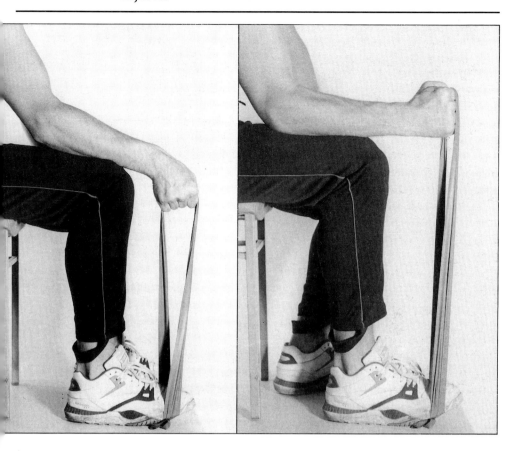

forces, as well as performing the most delicate of duties. To spring climbing on them when they're unprepared is asking for trouble. Because hand injuries are not totally disabling, they are often treated lightly, with a tendency to return to climbing before adequate healing has taken place.

There are several, quite common injuries that you ought to be aware of:

Collateral Ligament Sprains. These are the small ligaments that are on either side of your finger joints. They are usually damaged by a sudden sideways force to the finger, as in falling on a finger lock or monodoigt. Minor sprains cause tenderness over the side of the affected joint and pain on stressing the joint sideways. More serious tears leave the joint feeling 'wobbly' and, paradoxically, may be less painful than more minor injuries. If there is any doubt about whether the ligament is intact, a hospital opinion should be sought urgently, as complete tears are best treated by surgery. Minor tears can be treated by the usual first aid and the finger rested for two weeks by strapping it to the normal one next to it. Put a piece of gauze between them first, or they get very sweaty!

Tenosynovitis is an inflammation of the sheaths that the tendons run through. These sheaths normally provide a thin layer of lubricant, but when they become inflamed, this dries up, making movement of the tendons painful. There is often an associated 'creaking' sensation, which may even be audible, and the affected area is usually swollen. The most commonly affected area is the tendons over the back of the wrist, but the front of the wrist can also be affected and, more rarely, the individual finger tendons. The cause is overuse and the treatment is rest, best done by splintage. Non-steroidal anti-inflammatory drugs, steroid injections and ultrasound may also be useful.

Tendon Injuries. There are two tendons that bend each finger – one inserted into the base of the end bone, and one inserted into either side of the base of the middle bone. They can be injured together or individually, sometimes making recognition of the injury difficult. The seriousness of these injuries is not usually fully appreciated. Even partial tears should be treated with great respect if permanent damage and weakness are to be avoided.

Acute injury is most often caused by a fall on to bent fingers (or finger!) putting a sudden large force on to the tendons or tendon. It can also be caused by excessive strain, as in one or two-finger pull ups. Evidence seems to show that the ring finger is the most vulnerable to this sort of injury. With complete tears, there is often a 'snapping' sensation in the finger, accompanied by a good deal of pain. Pain may be felt at odd sites if the torn end of the tendon retracts into the palm. The finger may still move almost normally, due to the intact second tendon and only examination by someone who knows about hand injuries will reveal the full extent of the damage. IF THERE IS ANY DOUBT ABOUT A FINGER TENDON INJURY, A SPECIALIST OPINION SHOULD BE SOUGHT.

Complete tears are best treated by surgery within twenty-four hours of injury. Partial tears cause pain at some sites along the line of the tendon and pain on movement. Initial treatment is the standard first aid. Torn tendons take a minimum of six weeks to regain anything like full strength. After six weeks you should then slowly progress through a strengthening programme of exercises under supervision.

A2 Pulley Injury. This would appear to be the commonest acute injury to affect the hands of climbers who are climbing towards the limits that are now technically possible. This is the proper name for the 'pulled tendon'.

As the tendons run along the fingers they are held close to the bones by fibrous 'pulleys'. If this wasn't the case the tendons would 'bowstring' across the palm from wrist to fingertip every time you bent your finger.

These pulleys are vulnerable when 'crimping' (or in American, using the 'cling grip'), as the position of the fingers puts the pulley attached to the first bone of the finger – the A2 pulley – under enormous strain, and under extreme or shock loading it can fail.

There is often an audible snap, and there is pain and swelling at the base of the finger. Bruising may appear after twenty-four to forty-eight hours. Once this has settled there may be a feeling that the tendons 'bulge out' as the finger is bent. In extreme cases this may be visible (Fig 10).

Figure 10

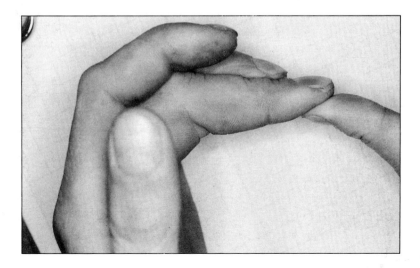

There is currently some debate as to the management of this injury. For minor tears the RICE regime and standard soft-tissue injury treatment with firm strapping of the base of the finger is perfectly satisfactory but it will be an average of three to five months before pain has settled and the finger can be retrained up to previous levels. For acute, complete tears, there is argument as to whether surgical repair has any advantage over more conservative measures. Certainly this is specialist surgery, so choose your surgeon carefully.

Taping around the base of the ring and middle fingers may help prevent this injury by providing an external support for the pulley (Fig 11). Two-and-a-half turns of 1.5 cm Zinc Oxide tape provide adequate support. Using tape has to be weighed against the possibility of getting it caught when falling, but this is probably a very small risk with most harder climbs.

Figure 11

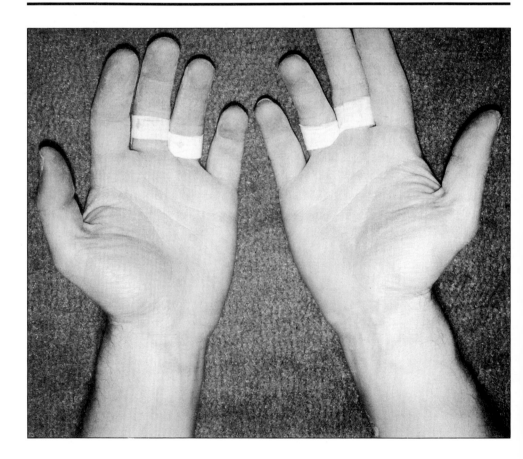

Tendonitis. This is a controversial area and much less common in finger tendons than elsewhere. Tendonitis implies an inflammatory condition of the tendons and this can be caused by incomplete healing of a partial tear or an overuse injury. It can affect any tendon in the body but, when it affects the tendons of the fingers, it is usually where one of the tendons that bends the finger inserts into the base of the middle bone.

Great care should be exercised with this condition. Chronic tendonitis is very difficult to treat and many top athletes have had their careers prematurely ended by this type of problem. It starts slowly, with pain occurring in a particular tendon after exercise. *This is the time to nip it in the bud.* Rest is vital. This doesn't mean the rest of the body has to lie idle, just avoid stressing the affected tendon.

As outlined above, a reduction in activity of 50 per cent may be all that is required at this stage. Non-steroidal anti-inflammatory drugs help settle associated inflammation. Don't let your finger or fingers set stiff while resting, but consciously bend and straighten them several times a day within the limits of pain. Start a gentle stretching programme as previously outlined. Progress carefully – you are not healed until you have returned to your previous standard and can perform maximally without pain.

The second stage of tendonitis is when pain persists during and for a few hours after exercise. If ignored, this progresses, with pain lasting longer and longer until it is more or less constant – stage four tendonitis. This requires prolonged rest and a long period of rehabilitation for which you need professional help. *Don't let it get this far!*

Flexion Contractures. Many top climbers have fixed deformities of the finger joints, with the first joints of the fingers permanently bent. This most commonly affects the ring and middle fingers. This probably occurs because, after heavy climbing/training sessions, the finger joints are mildly inflamed. Once you stop and rest, the fingers automatically adopt a curled up position. Unless the fingers are actively stretched out they 'set' in this position. The ring finger is most vulnerable because it is frequently used on small holds and is the most curled at rest. The little finger is rarely used on small holds and is therefore relatively unaffected.

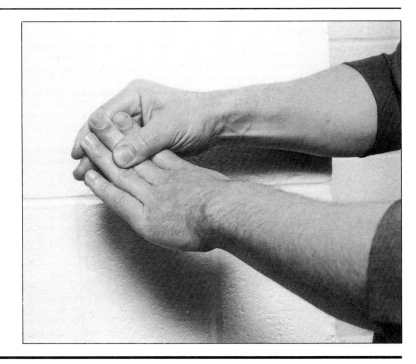

Figure 12

It is vital to actively stretch out the finger joints after climbing/training to try and prevent this occurring (Fig 12).

Arthritis. We know the development of arthritis is a multi-factorial problem and is not just the result of wear and tear. There is some evidence that the surfaces of joints can be conditioned to accept greater than normal loads, providing that these are built up over a prolonged period. Avoid spending too much time training on edges smaller than the end joint of your finger. This does nothing to improve tendon strength and knackers the joints. When training, avoid crimping where feasible, as this is associated with the largest force on the finger joints.

INJURY AND THE YOUNG

I think a special word must be said about the younger climber. I have seen children as young as five doing circuits on a climbing wall! Children and adolescents are by no means immune to the same overuse injuries as adults, usually from the 'too much over too short a time period' problem. In addition, they have some special problems of their own, both physical and psychological.

The skeleton does not reach full maturity until the late teens or early twenties. Until that time each bone in the arm and leg has growing areas at either end. These 'growth plates' are areas of potential weakness and may slip or fracture with a force smaller than that necessary to tear tendons or ligaments. This can occur through overtraining, especially weight training. It is therefore much more important to develop technique rather than power until growth has stopped.

Muscles, tendons and ligaments are particularly susceptible to injury during periods of growth and around puberty when, particularly in males, muscle bulk rapidly increases. At these times, there is an increase in muscle-tendon tightness around the joints and a loss of flexibility, increasing the chance of injury.

One often sees young athletes, in any sport, who are being pushed hard by their ambitious parents. Children are very susceptible to any sort of peer pressure. It is recognised that many of these children end up burnt out both physically and mentally, growing to hate both their sport and their parents. There is a very fine line between help and support and this kind of behaviour. As long as sport remains fun, though, there is little danger of overdoing it.

SPECIAL PROBLEMS OF WOMEN

It is well recognised that rigorous training in women, especially when associated with reduction in body fat, can cause disturbances in the menstrual cycle, either decreasing the frequency of or totally stopping periods (amenorrhoea). This problem is more likely to occur if under twenty-five years of age and if you have not previously had children and is experienced by many top female climbers.

While in itself this may not be seen as a problem, it is the secondary effects of a change in circulating hormones that may produce long-term effects on health.

We know that post-menopausal women suffer from a decrease in the density ('strength') of their bones, or 'osteoporosis', causing an increased incidence of fractures of one sort or another. In amenorrhoeic athletes, bony density is known to decrease and is associated with an increased incidence of stress fractures as well as the possibility of long-term problems. If you have been amenorrhoeic for six months and are not pregnant, you ought to think about doing something.

Initially, if you have a low body weight, you should aim to increase your weight by about 10 per cent (some top female climbers find that 2–3kg weight gain may make the difference) and to decrease your training by the same proportion over a period of about three to four months. This will restart periods in the majority of cases. If this fails or you are unwilling to alter your training programme, your hormonal status needs careful investigation and then treatment with hormonal replacement. See your doctor for a referral to an appropriate specialist.

DRUGS AND TRAINING

There is an old coaching saying, 'You can't put in what God left out', but thanks to the miracles of modern pharmacology this is perhaps no longer true. As the potential rewards grow, the temptation to speed up the processes of nature, or to give them a helping hand, may become very strong for some people. Drug taking to enhance performance is now widespread in such sports as athletics and bodybuilding.

All I can say to this is DON'T – for two reasons. Firstly it is cheating. It won't be you winning, it will be the biochemists. If you aren't naturally the best that's tough, all you can do is realise your full potential and give your best – no one can ask for more.

Secondly, and perhaps more importantly, it can be very dangerous for your health. Some of the commonly taken substances, such as anabolic steroids used to build up muscles quickly, are known to be a cause of cancer and other problems, like testicular atrophy.

Drug testing should now be an integral part of all major climbing competitions and a positive test will result in a ban of indefinite duration. A list of the substances banned or permitted by the International Olympic Committee can be obtained from the Sports Council.

It has recently been pointed out that, while ginseng root does not contain any banned substances, commercial preparations of it often contain other ingredients, such as ephedrine and a small amount of anabolic steroid. Other herbal preparations may contain banned substances that naturally occur in some plants, such as the Chinese plant Ma Huang, which could result in a positive test. There is currently no requirement for manufacturers to list the make up of these health supplements – so be careful.

PREVENTING INJURY

How do you prevent injury? This is what we all would like to know! 'If you don't want to get injured, don't climb' is the sort of standard quote a lot of climbers seem to get from their local doctor. To a certain extent this is true. Any athlete pushing him or herself to their limit is at risk of injury. When your body has nothing in reserve, it doesn't take much to tip the balance into injury. You can, however, minimise the chances of injury occurring.

Don't climb or train when tired, ill, inebriated or hung-over! Alcohol and its after effects, affect your judgement and coordination, as well as adversely affecting muscle function. You just think you can do better! Avoid exercise if you have a viral illness – viruses cause inflammation of your muscles (that's why you ache) and, as your heart is just another muscle, it also gets affected. There are many cases of fit young men dropping dead during exertion while having the flu.

There are two essentials in preventing injury – warm up and, surprise, surprise, training. A proper warm up is *vital* and is described elsewhere in this book. Training is what this book is about. A properly structured training programme will develop the strengths and skills that will help prevent injury. Sudden changes in intensity, duration or frequency of training are likely to cause injury. Overtraining is a temptation that should also be avoided. Rest is an important part of any training schedule and should not be forgotten. Your body needs time to recover from the punishments you subject it to (for instance, after a climb requiring maximum effort and endurance, it may take as long as seventy-two hours for your body to completely recover).

Vary your routines and exercises, so one group of muscles does not take all the strain in the same way each time. As previously described, most movements of the body are performed by pairs of muscles acting in opposite directions. If they are not in balance, excessive strain may be put on one set of muscles, leading to injury. Therefore, all training programmes should be aimed at providing balanced muscle development around each joint.

Care is needed particularly at the start of a training programme. Build up gradually. Muscles gain strength much more quickly than their tendons, and musculo-tendinous imbalance is a risk factor for injury. Beware of Bachar ladders and dead hangs. These forms of training are associated with a high incidence of serious injury.

If you are climbing hard routes it is advisable to put in some 'fall training'. If a fall is inevitable, it is much better to let go and control it (except if you're liable to deck it!) than to scrabble desperately at the rock, as this is liable to lead to injury. Falling 'safely' is an art and needs practice!

Lastly, a prominent climbing-injury expert from Switzerland suggests you should plan to achieve your maximum potential over a period of about four to six years in order to do yourself the least amount of damage, so you have plenty of time to reach the elusive 9A!

I hope this chapter hasn't turned you into a hypochondriac! Learn to listen to what your body is telling you and seek proper advice when necessary. There is no substitute for common sense where health is concerned. Above all, enjoy your training and climbing, after all, that's what it's all about, isn't it?

Suggested Further Reading

In the following short list of books you may find information which will be of use in planning your training programme.

Glass Bead Game, H. Hesse, Picador

Mental Training Programme, L. Hardy, J. Fazey, National Coaching Foundation (A series of cassettes and workbooks that deal with different aspects of mental training. Highly recommended.)

Physiology of Exercise: Responses and Adaptations, D. R. Lamb, Collier Macmillan

Roads to Freedom trilogy, J. P. Sartre, Penguin

Sporting Body, Sporting Mind: Athlete's Guide to Mental Training, J. Syer, C. Connolly, Simon & Schuster

Sports Fitness and Sports Injuries, Ed. T. Reilly, Faber & Faber

Stretching, B. Anderson, Pelham

Textbook of Science and Medicine in Sport, Ed. J. Bloomfield, P. A. Fricker, K. D. Fitch, Blackwell Scientific Publications

Walden, Henry Thoreau, Penguin

Zen and the Art of Motorcycle Maintenance, R. Pirsig, Vintage

Index

Page references to illustrations are underlined.

Index

Index